NEW ENGLAND ALCOS IN TWILIGHT

BY SCOTT HARTLEY

Foreword	2
1/The Alco diesel story	4
2/Class One lines	12
3/Visitors from the north	40
4/Short lines and newcomers	52
5/The future	70

NEW ENGLAND ALCOS IN TWILIGHT
From the publishers of PASSENGER TRAIN JOURNAL and PROTOTYPE MODELER

PUBLISHED BY
PTJ Publishing, Inc., Homewood, Ill., and Waukesha, Wis.

PUBLISHER
Kevin McKinney

PTJ BOOKS EDITOR
Mike Schafer

BOOK LAYOUT AND ART PRODUCTION
Mike Danneman

TYPESETTING
Publishers Studio, Waukesha, Wis.

HALFTONES, COLOR SEPARATIONS AND IMAGE ASSEMBLY
Jim Walter Graphic Arts, Beloit, Wis.

PRINTING
Tetra Print, Inc., Menomonee Falls, Wis.

©1984 by PTJ Publishing, Inc. All rights reserved. This book may not be reproduced in part or in whole without written permission from the publisher, except in the case of brief quotations used in reviews. Published by PTJ Publishing, P.O. Box 860, Homewood, IL 60430. Printed in U.S.A. ISBN: 0-937658-10-3. Library of Congress Catalog Card Number: 84-060963.

Cover scenes: Green Mountain RS1 No. 401 shuffles cars at Rutland, Vt., on a warm June day in 1981 (Mike Schafer); a Canadian Pacific Century 424 leans out of a bridge at Richford, Vt., in June 1983 (Scott Hartley); Maine Central 801 and 802—the road's only two RS11's—and Geep 565 idle away the evening hours at Bangor, Me., on Sept. 16, 1981 (Garland McKee).

This page: A Canadian National Bombardier HR412 and MLW M420R team up with three Central Vermont Alco RS11's to lead CV freight 444 across the Winooski River at Duxbury, Vt., Oct. 6, 1983. (Gary Knapp).

Ronald N. Johnson

All photos, except where indicated, Scott Hartley

Foreword

Why is it Alco locomotives are so popular among diesel enthusiasts? Perhaps it is simply because they are different. Through the decades, Alcos have toiled in relative obscurity among ubiquitous ranks of EMD covered wagons and hood units.

Alco's diesels *are* different. They're big and noisy and dirty. Often they emit large volumes of black smoke upon starting.

These same qualities that have endeared Alcos to trainwatchers have made the locomotives unpopular with some who have had to work on them. Railroaders will concede that an Alco will outpull any other engine in the roundhouse, but the admiration ends there. Engineers will complain of rough rides, and mechanics tell of the difficulties in repairing the locomotives.

But for those who enjoy watching trains, the Alco offers drama in today's world of sameness. With their smoke and noise, these engines are closer to steam power than anything else to be found running in regular service. And the happy part of the story is that they still can be found in regular service.

This book is not a comprehensive history of the Alco diesel in New England. Such an endeavor would require a volume several times this size. And since chapters are currently being added to the Alco story, the present is not the time to begin such a work.

The purpose of this book is to recognize that New England is not only a fine place to watch trains, but in the 1980's it's still a great region to see and hear the products of the American Locomotive Company or its Canadian counterpart Montreal Locomotive Works.

But Alcos are clearly in their twilight—even in New England. This book chronicles those twilight years, and should provide the incentive needed for those wishing to watch, ride, photograph, study, record and enjoy what is left of this dying breed.

In any work of this type, the input of a dedicated group of knowledgeable people is essential. I would like to thank the following historians and photographers for their generosity and assistance: Dave Albert, Jack Armstrong, T. W. Bossert, Charles A. Brown, Gary Carlson, Denis E. Connell, Bruce P. Curry, Ronald N. Johnson, Gary Knapp, Paul Lambert, Neal LeBaron, Garland McKee, Tom Nelligan, D. D. Perry, Tom Post, Roger S. Pugh, Maurice B. Quirin, J. J. Reddington Jr., Hal Reiser, Bob Richardson, Mike Schafer, J. W. Swanberg, Alan Thomas, and D. A. Woodworth Jr.

Scott Hartley
Waterbury, Connecticut
1983

303

7672
7672

MAINE CENTRAL
314

117

Amtrak
Amtrak

4221
4221
CP Rail
8400

Alco's first full-size, hooded diesel switcher, demonstrator 600, was sold to the New Haven Railroad in 1931. The pioneer is shown working Boston's South Station in April 1938.

Charles A. Brown

1/The Alco diesel story

The six states of New England have always been good places to watch Alco diesels. Of the major U.S. diesel locomotive builders, Alco's Schenectady, N.Y., headquarters was located closest to New England, and it seems logical that area railroads would patronize their local dealer.

But even in the mid-1980's, over a decade and a half after the last locomotive left Schenectady's erecting halls, in an era when diesel fans frequently travel hundreds of miles to photograph one rare unit, Alcos are still relatively abundant in New England.

The region's dependence on Alco locomotives dates back to the days of steam. Alco was the result of the 1901 conglomeration of steam builders Schenectady, Cooke, Dickson, Manchester, Pittsburgh, Rhode Island and Richmond, and the subsequent takeover of Rogers four years later. Engines from these plants would dominate New England rails until the end of steam.

As railroads became interested in internal combustion propulsion in the early part of this century, Alco participated in several projects, but usually just as the supplier of carbodies for other builders' tiny locomotives. Alco's first self-generated diesel locomotive project, and the country's first full-size hooded diesel switcher, was a 1931 600-h.p. demonstrator that was sold to the New Haven Railroad as its No. 0900. Subsequently, several additional diesels of similar design were sold to other Eastern railroads.

Alco's steam-minded management did take notice of these sales during those Depression years when the company had not received a single steam order. But as business improved in the late thirties, Alco once again was building steam locomotives, as well as its line of 600- and 900-h.p. diesels. Trade advertising by the company during those years boasted of the superiority of steam out on the road, but did acknowledge the availability of diesel switchers for efficient, high-utilization yard duties.

Just before the outbreak of the second World War, Alco introduced the 539 engine for its switcher line. A simple 6-cylinder, in-line design with a normal output of 660 h.p., and 1000 h.p. turbocharged, the 539 engine would serve the builder well in switchers (and the RS1 roadswitcher) through the late 1950's. Even at that early time, Alco was using fewer cylinders to produce the same horsepower as the competition.

With the advantage of hindsight, it seems easy to identify where Alco may have made its first big mistake. General Motors subsidiary Electro-Motive Corporation was already building diesel switchers and high-speed *Zephyr*s, and showing that a diesel-electric locomotive could handle the rigorous demands of Santa Fe's cross-country *Super Chief* schedule. By the late thirties, EMC was selling more of its standard E road passenger diesels than Alco was building switchers. This realization sent Alco management and engineers scurrying back to their drawing boards. Clearly, the demand had become greater than they had anticipated, and the company was not prepared to deal with these demands. A virtual duplicate to EMC's E unit was quickly introduced: the DL 109, with two 1000-h.p. 539 engines housed in a streamlined carbody riding on six-wheel trucks. The model sold a total of just 74 units, of

4

which 60 went to Alco loyalist New Haven, where they were used interchangeably in passenger and freight service.

General Electric, which supplied most of the electrical equipment used on Alco diesels, and American Locomotive signed a joint sales agreement in 1940, and for the next 13 years locomotives were marketed under the Alco-GE tradename. For the sake of simplicity in this volume, however, Schenectady-built diesel locomotives will be referred to as Alcos, regardless of their time of manufacture.

Electro-Motive, by 1939, already had its four-unit 5400-h.p. FT freight locomotive demonstrator on the road, and railroads were lining up for production models. Alco then belatedly set about designing a diesel engine for road locomotive use, but World War II intervened. The new War Production Board decreed that Electro-Motive would henceforth build only road locomotives, while Alco and Baldwin would be restricted to diesel switchers and steam locomotives.

This regulation undoubtedly was damaging to Alco's and Baldwin's futures as diesel builders. The companies could only watch helplessly as EMD, which in 1941 had become the Electro-Motive Division of General Motors, refined its 567 power plant while building hundreds of FT's for major railroads—companies which would be likely to continue to purchase a familiar product long after the war was over. One can only speculate as to what U.S. locomotive rosters would contain today if Alco or Baldwin instead had gotten the government nod for the manufacture of road diesels.

As the hostilities wound down, some of the WPB's restrictions were loosened, and Alco was permitted to field a three-unit 4500 h.p. road diesel demonstrator, containing new 241 model engines. The so-called "Black Maria" set, which included cabs that looked like a cross between the DL109 and Baldwin's later "Baby Face" designs, tested on the New Haven, Delaware & Hudson, Erie and Bangor & Aroostook in 1945-46. Although the experimental freighters pulled a record-setting number of cars on the BAR, it is reported that several breakdowns of the units marred the demonstration in Maine. Some observers suggest this was the reason BAR chose EMD when it later made its switch from steam to diesel.

When World War II ended, EMD definitely had the jump on Alco in the road diesel field—more than one thousand FT units were already working for American railroads. With production restrictions lifted, Alco

Roger S. Pugh

Following Alco's earliest slope-hooded designs, switchers were delivered in a variety of high-hooded formats through the remainder of the 1930's. **Above**, 531-powered Portland Terminal HH600 1004, built in June 1938, rides the turntable at Rigby Yard in South Portland, Me., July 24, 1971. Alco's switcher styling for the forties and fifties was the familiar boxy S-series. **Right**, 38-year-old PT S2 1051 rests between chores at Rigby's engine facility in 1980.

T. W. Bossert

Three photos, Scott Hartley

Alco-design locomotives have worn a variety of builder plates over the years. From top to bottom: Cast-iron Alco-GE plate from Penn Central (former-NH) RS3 5532, aluminum MLW plate on CP Rail RS18 8775 and Bombardier markings on Amtrak LRC 38.

faced the choice between utilizing the 241 engine or another new design, the 244. Reports indicated two separate factions within the company, each supporting one of the new prime movers. Oddly, the 244 engine was chosen by management even before the 241-powered Black Marias embarked on their demonstration tour, and the new prime mover was put into production with very little testing. Interestingly, the 244 was manufactured at Alco's Schenectady facility, while the 539 and later 251 were built at the old McIntosh & Seymour plant in Auburn, N.Y. Alco Engines Division of White Motor Corporation still manufactures 251 engines and parts at Auburn.

The V-16 244 engine, rated at 2000 h.p., was offered in the PA1 passenger locomotive, boasting as much horsepower from a single engine as two diesels generated in EMD's competitive E7. A 1500-h.p. V-12 244 powered the flat-nose FA freight cab units. But Alco showed itself to be a pioneer once again by putting the 1500-h.p. engines in a new carbody configuration, its four-axle RS2 and six-axle RSC2 roadswitchers. Baldwin introduced its own roadswitchers about the same time, without much sales success, but EMD didn't realize the value of the concept until three years later when it came out with the GP7. Alco usually gets recognition as creator of the roadswitcher design because of its 1941 introduction of the RS1, although many claim that this unit was simply an elongated switcher riding on road trucks. No one can argue that the postwar RS2's, generating the same tractive force as EMD and Alco streamlined freighters, were not true road units.

Despite brisk postwar sales, Alco still ran second behind EMD (with Baldwin, Fairbanks-Morse and Lima all plodding far behind). In retrospect, though, those postwar times were Alco's best in the diesel era. The company was out of the steam business within three years of the armistice. In 1947, Alco diesels accounted for 42 percent of all U.S. locomotive sales, the closest any builder has come to catching up with EMD, with the exception of a couple recent recession years when GE has actually outsold its LaGrange competitor. RS's, FA's and PA's joined the rosters of the majority of the nation's railroads in the late forties and early fifties. In New England, the New Haven, Rutland, New York Central's Boston & Albany and Canadian Pacific's Vermont lines were virtually all-Alco bastions. Boston & Maine and Maine Central preferred EMD's on the road, but did roster moderate collections of RS2's and RS3's and large numbers of Alco switchers. Portland Terminal amassed an all-Alco switcher fleet, and latecomers to the diesel world, such as Central Vermont and Grand Trunk, picked up a few Alco switchers and roadswitchers as their first non-steam power.

Unfortunately, the 244 line suffered from serious teething problems. Broken crankshafts and turbocharger failures were the most frequent maladies, and word of these difficulties spread quickly in railroad circles. By the time the problems were cured, Alco had already lost many actual and potential customers.

In the early part of this century, the American Locomotive Company had purchased a Canadian business that later became Montreal Locomotive Works. Beginning in 1948, even as Alco was selling off its interest in MLW, the Canadian firm began to build Alco-design diesels at its Montreal plant. Initially, MLW concentrated on 539-powered yard units—S-series switchers identical to those being produced at Schenectady. By 1950, though, Canadian roads had acquired a taste for diesels, and MLW expanded its output to include 244-powered FA and RS3 road units. Until 1961, MLW locomotives contained engines that had been manufactured by Alco in the U.S., and merely assembled in Montreal. At that time, MLW began building its own Alco-design diesel engines under license.

The Alco/General Electric sales agreement was dissolved in 1953, and GE set out on its own course of locomotive development that resulted in its U-Line and the eventual ouster of Alco from its position as the nation's Number Two diesel builder. However, GE continued to supply electrical equipment for Alco's locomotives, and this strange relationship continued until Alco's closing in 1969.

In 1951, Alco had set about to design a replacement engine for the trouble-prone 244. This program came to fruition in 1953, after a suitable period of development and experimentation, in the form of the 251. This prime mover was an evolutionary step from the 244. A bigger crankshaft and stronger main bearings eliminated most of the predecessor's failings. The first production-line 251's went into export locomotives and Boston & Maine's six S5's. Thirty years later, the basic 251 design is still at the heart of diesels being built in Canada by MLW's successor, Bombardier (pronounced bom-bar-dee-AY).

Until the introduction of the 251 engine, Alcos built north or south of the international border could be distinguished only by reading a unit's builder plate. Both Alco and MLW had sold a few 539 and 244 mod-

6

els that the other had not built, but carbody designs of both builders were usually identical. By the mid-fifties, however, Canadian interests had purchased a majority of MLW stock from Alco, and at about the same time differences in locomotive styles became quite noticeable.

In early 1954, with the introduction of the 2250-h.p. RSD7, Alco revamped its roadswitcher carbody designs by adopting an EMD-like high-hood configuration to accommodate the dynamic brake system over the engine and a steam generator in the short hood, as well as to allow installation of the anticipated new 251

Text continued on page 10

There is some debate in diesel circles whether or not Alco's 1941 RS1 was a true roadswitcher. Nevertheless, Green Mountain RS1 405 seems to be doing a fine job of handling the road's weekday local freight on a snowy morning in 1972.

Both photos, Scott Hartley

The postwar RS2 is more often credited as the first genuine roadswitcher, as it rode on the same trucks and had the same prime mover and generator as the FA1 road freight locomotive. Penn Central RS2 5229 arrives in West Springfield, Mass., with a traprock drag in the summer of 1972.

Alco's postwar road diesel offerings were round-hooded four- and six-axle roadswitchers and flat-nosed, grille-headlighted FA freight and PA passenger units. New Haven FA1 0428 and FB1 0456 await chores at South Boston, Mass., Aug. 13, 1968.

Scott Hartley

T. W. Bossert

Below, a pair of Amtrak RS3's is seen at New Haven, Conn., in the early morning hours of September 27, 1981. Diesel products of Alco and Montreal Locomotive Works were virtually identical until the mid-fifties, when new 251-powered units were introduced. Alco's 251 line of road locomotives featured deep notches in the hood corners, as shown on Maine Central RS11 801 at Bucksport, Me., in the summer of 1981, **right**.

Scott Hartley

U.S. Alcos were built with notched noses, but MLW's 251 line had featheredge hoods, resulting in a boxier appearance. **Below**, CP Rail 8784 at Brownville Jct., Me., Sept. 28, 1974, is an MLW RS18, the north-of-the-border equivalent of Alco's RS11. With the introduction of the Century-series locomotives, Alco designers eliminated the notches in favor of featheredges and angled windshields, as exemplified by Delaware & Hudson C420 406, **right**. Later freight offerings by MLW and today's Bombardier have featured wide noses and crew safety cabs, as shown by Canadian National M420R 2522, **lower right**.

Three photos, Scott Hartley

Both photos, Scott Hartley

Based solely on railfan appeal, Alco's PA passenger locomotive is probably the most popular diesel ever built. Regrettably for enthusiasts, PA sales amounted to fewer than 300 units, compared to more than 1,300 for competitor EMD's E units. **Above**, on the last day of PA passenger service in the U.S., Oct. 13, 1978, D&H PA 19 leads Massachusetts Bay Transportation Authority train 453 at Wellesley Farms, Mass. Today's Alco-engined passenger locomotive is Canada's Bombardier LRC. Amtrak sampled a pair of LRC consists for two years but did not purchase the trains. **Below**, in a rare meeting, both LRC engines are seen at New Haven, Conn., in January 1981.

prime mover. The new model also featured deep notches in the top corners of the short and long hoods. Later in 1954, MLW introduced the high-hood concept to its standard roadswitcher line with the debut of the 1600-h.p. RS10, essentially an RS3 without the classic rounded low hoods.

The Canadian difference was apparent in MLW's design, which didn't include Alco's notched noses, resulting in a boxier appearance. The styling of the 244-engined RS10 carried over to MLW's 251-powered RS18, while the RSD7's notched nose appeared on Alco's RS11. Despite the differences in appearance, the RS18 and RS11 are identical internally. The RS18, incidentally, would go on to become Montreal's all-time best seller, with 351 units built between 1956 and 1968.

With its 251 power plant, Alco had a tougher engine with lots of room for growth, and the company began to market locomotives with much greater horsepower than those of rival EMD. Unfortunately, U.S. locomotive sales were down to a mere trickle, as most railroads had just about completed their dieselization programs. It wasn't until a couple of years later that EMD boosted horsepower by adding turbochargers to its tried and true 567 engine, and actually began the horsepower war. By then railroads were ready to turn in their first diesels, and EMD's "unit reduction" principle—replace three old units with two new ones of higher horsepower—sounded good. And Alco, once more the pioneer, was doomed to disappointment as customers flocked to the competitor to purchase high-horsepower diesels.

Not many 251-engined Alcos went to New England railroads. Although Canadian-built RS18's were re-

The shadows are long at Penn Central's former-New Haven enginehouse at Hartford, Conn., on the evening of July 8, 1973. An S2 and several RS3's await the next morning's assignments as year-old EMD SW1500 9541 waits in the wings. By 1979, all of the Alcos had been retired.

Scott Hartley

sponsible for the final vanquishing of steam on the CPR in Maine, other local examples of early 251 units were rare, such as the six B&M S5's and two MEC RS11's. Even loyal Alco supporter New Haven was purchasing EMD's at the time, and only picked up 15 RS11's. New York Central 251 models came in on the Boston & Albany, but the new engine line was rare to the region indeed.

In those lean years of the late fifties, Alco had rebuilt its Schenectady plant, and concentrated on a lucrative export locomotive trade. It was during that time that the somewhat chauvinistic American Locomotive Company name was changed to Alco Products, Inc., perhaps in deference to the firm's best customers.

Alco's former minority competitors Baldwin and Fairbanks-Morse had stopped building locomotives for American railroads in the fifties, but the early sixties brought a strong challenge from former partner General Electric. GE's Universal series, led off by the U25B, quickly nudged Alco into the Number Three sales position.

In 1963, Alco once more rose to the challenge. The company's new Century line featured refinements to the existing mechanical layout and specifications, and a new appearance. With the introduction of the Centurys, MLW locomotives once again had the same appearance as those being built at Schenectady. The Centurys were distinguished from their predecessors by their feather-edge noses, slanted windshields and lack of hood louvers.

Soon after the Century's debut, Alco Products was purchased by long-time rail supplier Worthington Corporation, but the builder continued to operate as a separate entity. In 1967, the parent firm became Studebaker-Worthington. North of the border, Worthington and Studebaker-Worthington began to purchase MLW stock, and by 1967, had acquired a controlling interest. A year later, the Canadian builder changed its name to MLW-Worthington, Ltd.

The last Alco diesels built for a New England railroad were 10 Century 425's for the New Haven, delivered in the winter of 1964-65, at the same time the company was sampling an equal number of General Electric U25B's. Alco watched as its old-time friend went back to GE for an additional 16 units, and never returned to Schenectady.

Centurys built for New York Central and Pennsy would come into New England on the B&A and NH, which by the late sixties were part of the new Penn Central, and still younger freight units from survivor Montreal Locomotive Works would run on Canadian Pacific, Canadian National and, to everyone's surprise, the Providence & Worcester.

In fact, soon after Alco's exit from the business, MLW purchased its former parent's engineering designs and took over worldwide licensing agreements. MLW also announced its new M-series: essentially Centurys with many of the mechanical bugs worked out. MLW-Worthington was purchased by Bombardier, Ltd. (the same people who build snowmobiles) in the mid-1970's. In recent years, Bombardier has relied on export locomotive sales to stay open, but purchases by CN and VIA Rail Canada have been encouraging signs. A four-unit set of Bombardier's new "High Reliability" line of diesels demonstrating on CP Rail in 1983 offers hope to enthusiasts that there will be more chapters yet to write in the Alco story.

But in the U.S., by the late sixties, it was clear there was no room for a third locomotive builder. Higher horsepower units, reduction of passenger train service, and the growth of automated classification freight yards all had cut down on the need for locomotives, and EMD and GE were easily able to accommodate America's requirements. Alco shut its doors in January 1969, after the production of a couple of Newburgh & South Shore T6 switchers, with a boxy countenance not all that different from New Haven 0900 just 38 years earlier.

New Haven Railroad C425 2559 was the last Alco locomotive built for a New England railroad, delivered in January 1965. Six years later, the 2559 has become Penn Central 2459 and is seen leading a freight out of West Springfield, Mass., at sunset on a bitterly cold winter afternoon.

Scott Hartley

2/Class One lines

New England's Class I railroads were the best places to see Alcos in action. Despite the obvious attraction of a brightly painted switcher treading carefully down a weed-grown shortline right-of-way, only the big railroads could offer such sights as big Centurys heading up long tonnage trains, RS3's in both freight and passenger service, generous assortments of Alco switchers, and even flat-nose FA and PA cab units on the main line.

Sadly, by the late 1970's, most of these Alco stables had been put out to pasture. Today, active Alcos on New England's larger railroads are few and far between. This chapter studies the period from 1969 to the present, and puts in clear perspective what aficionados have lost with the retirement of Class I Alco fleets.

Penn Central and its successor, Conrail, presented the widest variety of diesels to be seen in New England during the twilight of the Alco. Unfortunately, an economic recession and large purchases of new locomotives in the late seventies combined to make Conrail an all-EMD and GE railroad by 1981. However, the array of models offered during the preceding 15 years made for interesting train-watching on these lines.

The New Haven Railroad and NYC's Boston & Albany Division, much of which today operates as Conrail lines, were rich in Alco heritage. The New Haven followed up its 1931 purchase of Alco's first 600-h.p. diesel switcher with repeated orders for successor models. The railroad operated 60 DL109 and 27 PA1 streamlined types in dual freight and passenger service, dieselized its important Maybrook freight line with A-B-A sets of FA's and assigned Alco roadswitchers and switchers to just about every other job. Despite minor inroads by other diesel builders (37 Fairbanks-Morse, 10 Lima, 2 Baldwin "Train-X" passenger sets and 54 General Electric units, including the railroad's final new diesel purchase of U25B's), Alcos reigned supreme. Number One diesel builder EMD did not succeed in placing a locomotive on New Haven's roster until the sale of 110 units of three models (FL9, GP9 and SW1200) between 1956 and 1960.

In later years, New Haven seemed to shy away from Alco products, sampling only 15 RS11's in 1956, and finally 10 C425's in 1964-65, the only 251-engined power on the railroad. Rumors abounded in the late sixties that NH would trade in its remaining 12 FA/FB's for a like number of Alco's center-cab C415 switchers, but the railroad's tight financial situation and the impending Penn Central takeover precluded this. The bankrupt New Haven Railroad was merged into the giant PC on Jan. 1, 1969, coincidentally just a couple of weeks before Alco built its last locomotive.

Despite the retirement of most of NH's earlier Alcos, the Schenectady-built locomotives nevertheless outnumbered those of any other builder on merger day. With takeover of the New Haven, Penn Central acquired interest in more than 130 Alcos, including models HH660, S1, S2, RS1, RS3, FA1, FB1, FB2, RS11 and C425.

The B&A line had an Alco heritage nearly as varied as that of the New Haven. The first diesels on the line were 11 high-hood Alco HH600's delivered in 1939 wearing B&A lettering, probably the only diesels to be so painted. Additional switchers from parent NYC arrived over the following years, and NYC's big push for dieselization after World War II brought road diesels onto the line.

Initially, just about every diesel model purchased by NYC could be found running on the B&A, with such exotic varieties as Baldwin Baby Face cabs, Fairbanks-Morse Erie-Builts and C-Liners, and Alco PA's all fighting the grades of the Berkshires. Before long, however, NYC began to assign the units of each builder to a specific area of its far-flung system, and the railroad's Alco locomotives became the bulwark throughout the Northeast.

Although rare Lima-Hamilton and Baldwin roadswitchers worked alongside Alco RS2's and RS3's in Boston commuter work, and EMD E7's and E8's were the preferred mainline passenger power over the entire NYC system, Schenectady-built products were the mainstay on the Boston & Albany. NYC's fleet of 197 FA/FB's and nearly-as-large collection of RS3's were the standard freight power on the line though the fifties and early sixties, while Alco switchers and roadswitchers held down local and yard chores.

The Central made small purchases of 251-powered RS11's and RS32's, which also appeared in later years, and the B&A remained virtually all-Alco until the invasion of EMD GP35's and GE U25B's beginning in 1963. NYC's last Alco purchase, 10 C430's in 1967, made occasional visits to New England, but by the time of the Feb. 1, 1968, Penn Central merger, the choice runs on the B&A main were under control of EMD and GE diesels.

Merger partner Pennsylvania Railroad had sampled more of Alco's recent offerings than the Central, having acquired 15 RS27's, 1 C424, 31 C425's, 15 C628's, 15 C630's and 15 C636's (the latter ordered by PRR, but delivered to PC). All PRR and NYC late-model Alcos (as well as second-generation EMD's and GE's) went into Penn Central's mainline freight power pool, and each model appeared on the Boston & Albany, with PRR's keystone, NYC's oval, and PC's "worms in love" schemes to be seen together and in profusion.

Former Pennsy six-axle power (notably absent on Water Level Route NYC's roster) found favor on the mountainous Boston & Albany, and big C-C Centurys, along with EMD SD's and GE's six-motor U-boats, all became common sights in Massachusetts. Alco switch-

The most common Alcos on Penn Central's New England lines were RS3's and S-series switchers of various New Haven, New York Central and Pennsylvania ancestries. **Above**, a pair of former-NH RS3's handles local switching at Manchester, Conn., Sept. 5, 1972. **Right**, an ex-NYC S2, still wearing a steam-era headlight visor, pulls a long cut of cars at West Springfield, Mass., May 30, 1970.

Both photos, Scott Hartley

ers and RS3's continued to hold yard and local assignments.

Upon the railroad's inclusion in Penn Central, New Haven's only second-generation power, 26 U25B's and the 10 C425's, became available to PC's mainline pool, but despite occasional wanderings to the west, these units spent most of the years following the merger on home rails and on the B&A.

Penn Central management in Philadelphia was perfectly content to leave New Haven's aged Alco fleet operating on the property of its unwanted foster child. Ex-PRR RS3's were sent to New England, to permit the retirement of the most decrepit of NH's undermaintained roster. Other New Haven power, however, rolled on, wearing new PC numbers, and frequently, coats of shiny black paint. Relics including several RS1's, a handful of FA's and FB's, and even one HH660, carrying PC number 9411, ran into the early 1970's.

Joining these unusual species on former-NH rails were other odd ex-Pennsy Alcos. Penn Central RS3

Text continued on page 16

13

A remarkable assortment of elderly New Haven Alcos found themselves on the Penn Central roster in 1969. **Upper left**, NH HH660 0924 became PC's only high-hood, surviving until 1971; it is shown at South Boston in 1969. **Left,** S2 9859 (ex-NH 0618) works for subsidiary Union Freight Railroad on street trackage along Boston's Atlantic Avenue in October 1969. **Above**, an A-B-A lashup of ex-NH Alco cabs rolls freight BL-1 through Medfield Junction, Mass., during an October 1969 snowstorm.

All photos, Tom Nelligan

PC 9946 at Providence in late 1969 is one of six New Haven RS1's that made it into the merger.

Tom Nelligan

Tom Nelligan

Scott Hartley

All 25 of New Haven's 251-powered Alcos were included in PC's roster. **Above**, C425's are at A Street in South Boston in 1972. **Top**, an ex-NH RS11 leads a GP30 and an RS3 at Medfield in May 1972. Big treats for New England Alco fans were the arrivals of six-axle Alcos from the Pennsy. **Top right**, 6811, one of two RSD15's assigned to former-NH lines for a couple of years after the merger, switches at Providence in 1969. **Right**, C630 6327 teams up with GE's and a GP30 to move westbound B&A tonnage over the Berkshires near Dalton, Mass., in January 1970.

Tom Nelligan

Above, in a rare passenger appearance, former-NH RS11 7673 leads New York-bound Penn Central train 83 out of Springfield, Mass., in July 1969. **Right**, Penn Central's last RS2, 5229, passes the station at Stockbridge, Mass., on the ex-NH Berkshire Line in October 1974.

5569, one of a kind on the PRR (four similar units were owned by the Western Maryland), with a high short hood housing both a steam generator and dynamic brakes, came in 1969, as did a pair of RSD15's, six-axle giants which went to work at Cedar Hill and Providence. All of these rarities were gone by the early seventies.

Under the merger, New Haven's traditional traffic routes in and out of New England via New York City car floats and the Maybrook freight line were eliminated in favor of moving trains over the B&A to and from ex-NH points. The resulting run-through of motive power bumped former-NH engines off symbol freights, with RS11's and even some C425's demoted to local freight chores, which in turn pushed many RS3's into yard service.

More bad news for Alco fans came in early 1972 when approximately half of the PC's order of 40 EMD SW1500's were assigned to New England lines. The tall, husky switchers, along with reassigned ex-NH SW1200's, replaced most of the RS3's, S2's and S4's along the B&A. By 1973, it was difficult to find any Alco on this line that had been the exclusive domain of these diesels just a decade earlier. A few SW1500's went to work out of former-New Haven terminals, similarly leaving RS3's and S1's unemployed.

Two notable Alcos did appear in New England in the early 1970's when ex-NYC RS2's 5212 and 5229 were transferred to the B&A line. They were the last examples of this model on Penn Central's huge roster, and ran on locals out of Springfield and Pittsfield, even as younger RS3's went to the scrapper. The 5229 was finally retired in 1975.

Penn Central's six-axle Centurys and 10 C430's were removed from the mainline pool in 1972, moving to Ohio to handle mineral traffic and transfer duties. Ex-Pennsy C425's, RS27's and the C424 were likewise reassigned to freight service in the Pittsburgh area.

In its final years as a railroad, Penn Central did not offer much encouragement to Alco-watchers in New England. All that broke the EMD/GE monopoly were the ex-NH RS11's and C425's, working in local service, and dwindling numbers of RS3's and 660- and 1000-h.p. switchers of various origins. In 1975, even the 10 ex-NH Centurys were sent to Ohio.

At the same time, the sound of many of the Alco locomotives was changing as PC began to re-engine RS3's with EMD 1200-h.p. engines at its DeWitt Shops in Syracuse, N.Y. The "DeWitt Geeps" began arriving in New England in the mid-seventies, and each time an additional rebuild appeared, one more RS3 would vanish.

During the early 1970's, Penn Central abandoned several former New Haven low-density branch lines, putting more Alcos out of work. Beginning with the 1973 independence of the Providence & Worcester, new operators have taken over many other former-NH

16

segments of PC, and later, Conrail, trackage. Happily, some of these new operations have utilized Alco diesels to move their trains. These railroads are covered in chapter 4.

The conveyance of Penn Central's rail assets to Conrail on April 1, 1976 brought further changes to New England's Alco lineup. First, 45 RS3's of various NYC, PRR and NH ancestry were transferred to Amtrak ownership (see page 21). But even with this large loss of Alco power, Conrail still had 178 RS3's and 17 RS2's from the rosters of Penn Central, Central Railroad of New Jersey, Erie Lackawanna and Lehigh Valley. Following the tradition of Penn Central, Conrail's Motive Power Control assigned the giant railroad's Alco fleet to the northeast quarter of its system.

Three Erie Lackawanna units—a pair of RS3's and a single RS2—were transferred to Connecticut in the summer of 1976, and the gray-and-maroon Alcos could be found in yard and local service out of Hartford and New Haven for nearly a year. CR also continued PC's practice of retiring 539-engined Alcos, and soon after conveyance day, New England's remaining S's were reassigned to yards in the swamps of New Jersey, where they ran their final miles over the next couple years.

The 13 remaining ex-NH RS11's received new numbers on Conrail's roster, and a handful even received full blue paint jobs. (No Conrail RS3 or 539-engined switcher ever was painted blue.) Their final home was Cedar Hill (New Haven), and before retirement in 1978-79, they could be found switching the yard there, or on locals on the Shore Line and up the Norwich Branch.

Although Conrail wasted no time sending LV's and RDG's big Centurys to Ohio for ore assignments, RDG and EL C424's remained in general freight service, and could be seen from time to time on CR freights in Massachusetts and Connecticut.

During slow traffic periods, and after they were replaced in mineral service in 1979, Conrail's C628, C630 and C636 types also appeared in New England on a few rare occasions.

Conrail continued re-engining RS3's with EMD power plants, first at DeWitt and later at Altoona, Pa., and the rebuilds replaced more "pure" Alcos in Connecticut. By the late seventies, more than a dozen RS3m's could regularly be found working out of Hartford and New Haven.

Text continued on page 20

A common disposition for Penn Central's and Conrail's RS3's was to re-engine them with EMD prime movers. Left, five of these so-called "DeWitt Geeps" arrive in Springfield, Mass., with a freight up from New Haven in early 1977.

Neal LeBaron

T. W. Bossert

Alcos were rather short-lived on Conrail's roster, and the big railroad did not bother to paint many into its blue colors. Right, three RS11's are on the point of tonnage on the old NH Norwich & Worcester line in 1977. This trackage belongs to the Providence & Worcester today.

Perhaps the most versatile of Penn Central's Alcos were the RS3's. Though mostly assigned to freight duties, such as on the North Adams (Mass.) local, **right**, at Cheshire, Mass., in 1970, RS3's also held down Boston commuter assignments until 1972. **Below**, the 5527 rolls passengers through Needham Centre in August 1971.

Tom Nelligan

Tom Nelligan

Scott Hartley

Yard duties were common, too, for the RS3's. Former PC 5480 is working at Manchester, Conn., in December 1976 during Conrail's infancy.

By the 1970's, the appearance of RS3's in road freight service had become increasingly rare. Here a pair of former PRR units rattle the diamond at Walpole, Mass., in August 1969.

Tom Nelligan

J. W. Swanberg

J. W. Swanberg

Scott Hartley

Conrail inherited from Penn Central 13 of the original NH RS11's, renumbered them, and kept the units mostly in Connecticut. **Above left**, a trio of RS11's show off their notched noses at Cedar Hill Yard in October 1977. **Right**, RS11 7598 and two GE's move a short train past Hawleyville Tunnel on the old NH Maybrook line in autumn 1977. **Left**, Conrail reassigned three ex-Erie Lackawanna RS's to Connecticut. One is shown working the "Roustabout" at Hartford yard in July 1976.

During Conrail's first couple years, the huge railroad was constantly short of operational locomotives, and one makeshift solution deserves attention in this volume. Motive power managers noticed that a great many yard and local freight engines sat idle on weekends, and it seemed logical to make better use of these locomotives. Beginning in late 1976, four or five Hartford units would be lashed together every Friday night, and spend Saturdays and Sundays hauling symbol freights. The usually assigned engines were the RS3m DeWitt Geeps, but RS11's and RS3's were used on many occasions. The weekend teams were unsuccessful on the grades of the B&A, but performed satisfactorily on the New Haven-Springfield line, and five-unit sets of RS3m's were regular sights along the Connecticut River for more than a year.

But as Conrail began acquiring new locomotives and rebuilding long-neglected older units, Alcos were rapidly set aside for retirement. DeWitt Geeps, and EMD switchers and GP units, replaced the remaining RS3's and RS11's by 1979. Systemwide, products of General Motors and General Electric killed off the final examples of Conrail's predecessors' once expansive Alco stable.

The only operating CR Alcos to survive into this decade were five former-NYC passenger-equipped RS3's, all assigned to CR's Metropolitan Region out of Harmon, N.Y. These venerable Alco-GE's, built in 1951, were available as commuter protection power, but spent most of their time switching coach yards and on work and wire trains. The last runs of a Conrail Alco in New England came in late 1980, when RS3 5507 held down the wire train assignment out of Stamford, Conn. All five units were retired soon after, forever silencing Alco engines on Conrail.

As a postscript, even those RS3's rebuilt with EMD engines are in danger. With traffic down due to the continuing recession, Conrail has retired some unserviceable DeWitt Geeps, and by 1983, all of the remaining units were in storage. Without a major upswing in the economy, the RS3m's could be prime candidates for trade-in or sale on the used-locomotive market.

Metro-North Commuter Railroad, a subsidiary of New York's MTA, took over control of Conrail's commuter lines in Connecticut and New York on January 1, 1983. The new company acquired from Conrail 33 FL9 electric/diesel-electrics, hundreds of coaches and elec-

Scott Hartley

Common MTA ownership of Long Island Rail Road and Metro-North Commuter Railroad has resulted in LIRR C420's being assigned to Connecticut and New York MNC lines. Number 225 prepares to leave Waterbury, Conn., with a ballast train Aug. 8, 1983.

Still clad in its New York Central scheme, now PC-owned RS3 5295 heads northbound local SX-8 along the ex-NYC North Adams branch at Lanesboro, Mass., on Feb. 19, 1968.

Jack Armstrong

Both photos, Scott Hartley

For a company born more than two years after Alco's closing, Amtrak has managed to acquire a great deal of Alco expertise. At **right**, the fireman on a Bombardier LRC trainset waits for the highball at New Haven in April 1982. **Above**, a pair of RS3's moves a train of orange ballast hoppers through Hartford, Sept. 25, 1977.

tric m.u. cars, and several roadswitchers for work train service, including one "DeWitt Geep." MNC 605, still in Conrail blue but with all markings painted over, was probably the last unit of its type to be operating in late 1983.

The big surprise for Connecticut and New York trainwatchers in the summer of 1983 was the arrival of two Alco C420's from Metro-North's sister MTA road, the Long Island. The big blue and white Centurys, with high short hoods and special high-adhesion trucks, were built just five months before Alco's demise, and had spent several years in high-speed passenger service. Metro-North has used them in a variety of work train functions, and the sounds of 251 engines have once again become familiar along former NH and NYC iron.

When Amtrak took over the nation's intercity passenger trains in May 1971, no one thought the new company would be an operator of Alco diesels. After all, the builder had closed its Schenectady plant two years earlier, and EMD and GE had passenger diesels in their respective catalogs. Besides, railroads owned hundreds of EMD E and passenger-equipped F-units that were all looking for new homes.

Amtrak did the expected, by purchasing the best of the private railroads' E's and F's as well as a selection of GG1 electrics. One Alco did show up in Amtrak's platinum mist paint in the early seventies—a former-U.S. Army S2, which still works side by side with the blue RS1's of the Washington Terminal Company at Washington Union Station. And Alco-design MLW units belonging to Canadian National will wander as far south as New Haven on the occasions that the *Montrealer*'s power fails at the north end of its journey. But what no one predicted in 1971 was that in five years Amtrak would acquire title to the tracks and right-of-way of America's busiest passenger line, the Boston-New York-Washington Northeast Corridor.

With its own railroad came the need for additional locomotives, particularly engines to power work trains for the planned rebuilding of the Corridor track. Meeting that need were 45 RS3's of various Pennsylvania, New York Central, and New Haven ancestry. Several members of this tired fleet had been already stored unserviceable by Penn Central, but Amtrak was able to make at least three-quarters of them run, and by the late seventies these units had become North America's largest stable of RS3's.

The Alcos not only performed admirably in work train service, but have paid for their keep handling terminal switching duties, and frequently rescuing disabled diesel and electric trains on the road. The RS3's have retained their PC-style utilitarian black paint scheme.

Twenty secondhand GP7's and GP9's also arrived on the Northeast Corridor in 1978, casting the first shadow of doubt as to the future of the RS's. The rebuilt bright orange Geeps allowed the retirement of the worst of the RS3's. And further bad news was the installation of an EMD prime mover in one RS3 in 1981. Two more units received this treatment two years later, and although it is expected that the remainder of the 244 engine fleet will follow in the future, about 15 pure RS3's remained on the roster in late 1983.

An even bigger surprise than the RS3's was the two-year demonstration of Bombardier's LRC on Amtrak's Boston-New York line. Two of these new generation Canadian trainsets, each pulled by a 251-powered streamlined locomotive, worked in revenue service on the former New Haven Shore Line from 1980 to 1982.

Text continued on page 24

21

At **left**, LRC 38 gets its face washed at New Haven Motor Storage in April 1982. **Above**, a two-car westbound *Beacon Hill* minutes out of Boston stops at Route 128 station in March 1981.

Tom Nelligan

Scott Hartley

LRC 38 again, this time reposing with much older Alcos at New Haven Diesel Shop in September 1980. Below, another of Amtrak's Alco experiences is the periodic visit of Canadian National passenger RS18's when the *Montrealer*'s power fails north of the border. CN 3116 passes an Amtrak AEM7 at New Haven on one such occasion, May 8, 1983.

Scott Hartley

Scott Hartley

Amtrak's RS3's have proven invaluable for a multitude of chores. At **left**, number 100 switches the *Lake Shore Limited* at Boston South Station in 1980. **Above**, RS3 104 and E8 496 handle a "tow job"—the hauling of trains in electrified territory due to reduced overhead power—at New Haven, April 9, 1981.

Below, three Alcos rip through Stamford, Conn., at dawn on Aug. 30, 1980, with an eastbound Amtrak ballast train. **Right,** former NH 138 at rest in New Haven in 1983.

Scott Hartley

Below, Boston & Maine and Vermont Railway RS3's meet at North Bennington, Vt., Feb. 3, 1975. **Above**, B&M S2 1265, wearing the road's maroon road-unit paint scheme, works at East Deerfield, Mass., in 1970. **Right**, S4 1271, which in a few months would become the last active B&M Alco, switches at East Deerfield in September 1979.

Scott Hartley

Jack Armstrong

The high-speed train with its sophisticated power-banking system performed well on the serpentine route, and Amtrak was impressed. Unfortunately for Bombardier and Alco fans alike, the timing was poor. Amtrak was on the verge of finally having a standardized equipment roster, and at the same time, was facing budget cuts from a hostile Administration in Washington. It was not a good time for the company to be purchasing unusual equipment. Thus, when their lease expired in April 1982, the two trains returned to their Montreal birthplace.

Even without these speedy Canadians, however, the Northeast Corridor main and the New Haven-Springfield line remain fine places to view RS3's in regular action, and are still New England Alco capitals.

The Boston & Maine expressed an early interest in internal combustion with its 1934 purchase of a 600 h.p. Alco diesel switcher. This first locomotive was followed by a pair of diesel railcars, a GE switcher, and in conjunction with Maine Central, an Electro-Motive stainless-steel streamliner patterned after Burlington's *Pioneer Zephyr*.

Hal Reiser

Very early the B&M became partial to the products of Electro-Motive Corporation, and its successor, General Motors' Electro-Motive Division. By the late forties, EMD switchers and E and F road units could be found in profusion, with handfuls of Alco switchers and GE 44-tonners working in comparative obscurity.

In 1949, Boston & Maine acquired its first Alco road diesels, in the form of 10 RS2's. Later orders of RS3's through 1955 brought an additional 26 round-hooded Alcos to the road. Most of these were steam generator-equipped, and they spent their early years in secondary passenger and local freight service on B&M's eastern end.

A healthy number of 539-engined switchers joined the roster in the forties and fifties, including 10 S1's, 6 S2's, 16 S3's, and 8 S4's. (A fire-damaged S3 was later rebuilt to an S4 by Alco.)

Like many other railroads, Boston & Maine painted its first diesels in basic steam locomotive black. Later, road diesels were delivered in B&M's classic maroon with gold striping, and switchers received the addition of red and white trim on their black bodies. Many exceptions existed, such as switchers intended for branchline work which were painted maroon, and pioneer RS2 1500 which wore the black switcher scheme.

An order of 50 GP9's from EMD in 1957 (followed by six GP18's in 1961) introduced the blue, black, and white "Bluebird" scheme to the railroad, but with the exception of a few blue F's and one S4, it wasn't until the late sixties that other units began to routinely receive solid blue paint jobs. Since that time, all B&M units have carried some version of the solid blue, although it is expected that future repaints will be in the gray of new owner Guilford Transportation Industries.

Boston & Maine's only sampling of Alco's 251 engine line came in 1954 (a year before the last two RS3's) in the form of a half-dozen S5's. These 800 h.p. switchers apparently were not a great success, as four were upgraded to 1000 h.p. by the railroad. All six spent most of their lives in the Boston area, and were out of service by the mid-seventies. Surprisingly, two of these rare Alcos still sat rusting outside B&M's Billerica, Mass. shops in the early eighties.

Despite its fair representation on B&M's roster, Alco did not sell a single diesel to the railroad in the last 14 years of the builder's existence. EMD's held down the hotshot road jobs, but Alco switchers were common sights across the system. Following their replacement by Budd RDC's in most commuter and local service,

Right, MBTA Boston-bound commuter train at Weston, Mass., May 31, 1978, is led by leased Delaware & Hudson PA 16. **Above,** Guilford Transportation Industries' takeover of B&M, MEC and D&H has brought the latter road's Alcos into New England. A D&H C424m works with two smoking MEC GE U25B's on a B&M freight at Greenfield, Mass., May 28, 1983.

Scott Hartley

Jack Armstrong

Scott Hartley

Scott Hartley

Upper left, B&M RS3 1506 pushes an eastbound freight through Millers Falls, Mass., July 13, 1973. **Upper right**, 1519, the last Alco purchased new by the B&M, is in the power consist of a Mechanicville-bound freight at East Deerfield on a rainy Thanksgiving 1975. **Left**, two of B&M's 251-powered S5's are seen at Boston Engine Terminal in 1972.

the RS2's and RS3's went to work hauling freight trains on secondary lines. Their favorite haunts were out of White River Junction, Vermont, south to Springfield, Mass., and southeast to Boston. Through the sixties and early seventies, the RS's could be found on those lines, keeping company with the last of B&M's once-large F-unit fleet.

As branchlines were abandoned, and new EMD's arrived on the property, the RS3 count dwindled to less than 10 units by the early seventies. And those Alcos were frequently leased out to power-hungry neighbors Delaware & Hudson and CP Rail. The road's first RS2, 1500, which was built without m.u. capability and thus escaped years of grueling road freight work, held down local freight assignments in Massachusetts and New Hampshire, and was a photographer's favorite until its retirement in 1975.

Alco fans were given an unexpected gift when B&M received two "new" RS3's in 1974. Delaware & Hudson, in need of passenger diesels to power its new Amtrak Albany-Montreal train, swapped a pair of its RS3's for two of B&M's steam generator-equipped Alcos. The D&H units arrived in fresh B&M blue paint, carrying the numbers of the engines they replaced, 1508 and 1536. (They were later renumbered 1547 and 1546.) The two proved to be breakdown-prone, and to add to their woes, they wouldn't operate with other B&M diesels. The two spent their few years in service leased back to the D&H, or working in pusher and local service on the western end of the railroad.

An order of 18 GP40-2's in 1977 freed up enough older EMD's to replace most of the few remaining Alcos. A pair of S4's survived into early 1980, one working at East Deerfield, Mass., the other leased to the Portland Terminal at Rigby Yard.

Although the Boston & Maine of this decade is an all-EMD railroad, this does not mean that Alcos are gone from the property. Oddly, various power pools and the road's consolidation into Guilford Transportation Industries have been responsible for bringing quite a few Alcos onto the B&M.

Various Delaware & Hudson, Erie Lackawanna, and Penn Central Alcos came into New England on the B&M as the result of power runthrough agreements in the late sixties and early seventies. Visits of EL power were shortlived, the D&H pools were instituted and cancelled with regularity, and Alcos grew scarce and finally non-existent on PC (later Conrail) pool trains later in the seventies. It was Canadian Pacific (with RS3's, RS10's, RS18's, and C424's) and Central Vermont (with RS11's) that contributed Alco-design diesels to the B&M's Connecticut River line through the late seventies and early eighties. Those pools have been terminated, but on rare occasions, CP and CV Alcos still show up south of White River Junction.

26

An interesting collection of D&H Alcos began running regularly on the Boston & Maine in 1982, as these four views attest. **Above,** Mechanicville-Portland freight MEPO nears Hoosac Tunnel behind a C420/C424m/U23B lashup, and is seen bursting out of the east portal of the 4.75 mile bore, at **left**. RS3u 508, **right**, is on the point of symbol LAME at Zoar, Mass., on Aug. 8, 1982. **Below left**, D&H C420 410 (an ex-Lehigh Valley unit wearing an unusual notched nose received from an ex-N&W RS11 during wreck rebuild) powers B&M local ME-2 on B&M's ex-CR(NYC) Adams Branch, Nov. 6, 1982.

All photos, Jack Armstrong

Scott Hartley

Scott Hartley

Cooperative management of Boston & Maine and Maine Central until the mid-1950's resulted in the similar paint schemes worn by B&M, MEC and sibsidiary Portland Terminal diesels. On this page, B&M's early black-and-red switcher colors are seen on Alcos of all three roads. **Left**, B&M S4 1267 pulls a cut at East Deerfield in October 1970. **Below**, MEC S1 957 brings a carload of fish feed off the Eastport branch at Perry, Me., in the summer of 1978. **Above**, PT S1 1008 works yard 8 in Portland, March 16, 1975.

Tom Post

Although fans decry the immersion of B&M into Timothy Mellon's Guilford B&M/MEC/D&H triumvirate, the combined operations of the three railroads have brought Alcos (and GE's) into the exclusive EMD domain of the Boston & Maine mainlines. Beginning in 1982, Delaware & Hudson Alcos of such varied models as RS11, RS36, C420, C424m, and RS3u have been seen rolling through Massachusetts, New Hampshire, and Maine.

The Alcos do not have a long life expectancy once Mellonization is complete, but for the time being, 251 engines have added a new echo to be heard coming from the depths of Hoosac Tunnel.

During the 1970's, the Massachusetts Bay Transportation Authority assumed control of Boston area rail commuter service by purchasing the trains and the tracks they ran on from Boston & Maine and Penn

Maine Central's Alco road units spent most of their lives working on the eastern end of the railroad. **Left**, half of Maine Central's RS11 fleet, the 801, rests at Rockland, Me., on a July evening in 1978. **Above**, an RS3/GP38 duo prepares to depart eastward from Bangor in July 1974.

Mike Schafer

Garland McKee

Hal Reiser

MEC 802—sister to 801—and a Geep bring a Bucksport job across the Penobscot River at Bangor, June 16, 1983. **Below**, RS2 554, in an experimental paint scheme, and RS3 556 are at Calais, Me., Oct. 7, 1974.

Ronald N. Johnson

MEC's two RS11's in old colors are underneath threatening skies at Waterville in December 1973.

Maine Central's m.u.-equipped S4's spent much time in their later years working Bangor-Bucksport freights. **Left**, the 314 and 313 lead the First Bucksport Extra at Bucksport in September 1980. **Above**, S1 957 poses in front of the tiny enginehouse at Livermore Falls, Me., on a rainy June 10, 1972.

Central. Both railroads (and PC's successor, Conrail) were contracted to operate MBTA trains on their respective territories until 1977, when B&M took over operations of all suburban service.

MBTA's equipment roster was composed of a motley collection of former B&M and NH Budd RDC's, ex-PRR E8's, and ex-NH GP9's. This fleet was well past its prime, and the agency was frequently forced to lease B&M and Amtrak locomotives to aid its own tired engines. Boston & Maine Geeps and Amtrak E's were the most common, but Amtrak's Alco RS3's could be found quite often on former-NH routes, especially during major snowstorms.

The MBTA had arranged to acquire new and rebuilt locomotives, but in the meantime, the agency arranged a lease that was to become the biggest treat in years for New England Alco fans. Arriving in Boston in late September 1977 were Delaware & Hudson's four PA's. These former-AT&SF beauties, recently rebuilt, had been bumped from D&H's Amtrak run the preceding winter, and placed in storage after a few months in freight service. MBTA quickly put the much-needed power on the road, and for the next year the PA's flat noses and grilled headlights graced the old NH and B&A lines out of South Station.

The big Alcos were breakdown-prone in the winter, and during the cold months were commonly m.u.'ed with MBTA E8's. But the summer of 1978 was a great time to watch and hear PA's loping along with trains of stainless-steel ex-New Haven coaches, 15 years after such sights had been dismissed as memories of the past.

The stay of the PA's in New England was cut short by their owner's worsening financial plight. The D&H, in desperate need of cash, arranged a sale of 37 of its locomotives, including the four PA's and 18 big Alco C628's, to an equipment broker for use in Mexico.

The last four PA's in existence made their final American revenue passenger runs on Friday the thir-

Upper left, Maine Central's two RS3's round a curve near Mattawamkeag, Me., with Vanceboro-Bangor train VB-2 in 1969. **Below**, RS3 557 has been repainted in a simpler scheme as it pauses at Ayers Junction, Me., en route from Calais to Bangor in 1974. **Above**, in their final months of regular service, S2 303 and S1 960 work side by side at Waterville in September 1980.

teenth of October, 1978, and two days later were returned to the Delaware & Hudson. With purple and gray F's and F40's, MBTA trains are pleasing to view, but Boston trainwatchers still regret the passing of the four blue Alcos.

The Maine Central has always been considered a General Motors railroad, not surprising in view of the fact that mainline operations were dieselized for the most part by 7 E7's, 20 GP7's, and 10 F3's. However, well before the arrival of the first E7 in 1946, Maine Central and subsidiary Portland Terminal had been sampling Alco's line of diesel switchers.

Following the joint MEC/B&M *Flying Yankee* streamliner built by Electro Motive in 1935, Maine Central's first diesels were a pair of high-hood HH660's, delivered in 1939. These were followed by periodic purchases of Alco's 660 and 1000 h.p. switchers during the 1940's and early 1950's. Ten S1's and S3's replaced elderly 0-6-0 steam locomotives throughout the system, and 10 stronger S2's and S4's (all but two equipped for multiple unit operation) found their way into local and helper service.

With these 22 Alco switchers appearing over the length of the system, MEC's total of five EMD SW7 and SW9 switchers indeed were a minority.

On the road, however, General Motors was clearly the victor. All of those Geeps and covered wagons were conspicuous on the best varnish and hotshot symbol freights. MEC never purchased a Schenectady-built cab unit, and finally acquired its first Alco road units in the form of of five RS2's in 1949. A pair of RS3's arrived in 1953, and the seven round-hooded road-switchers spent most of their lives working north and east of Bangor, far from the glamour assignments of their EMD cousins.

The Maine Central's last purchase of Alco diesels came in 1956 with the delivery of two 251-powered 1800 h.p. RS11's (one of the two was initially lettered Portland Terminal, but the unit was officially transferred to the MEC less than a year later). The RS11's spent many years together, working wood trains on various runs out of Waterville and Bangor, but by the early 1970's could be found with EMD's in the regular road power pool.

When delivered, Maine Central's Alcos wore paint schemes based on the colors of cooperative-management partner Boston & Maine, the classic maroon and gold for road units, and black with red nose stripes on

31

Above, two Portland Terminal S4's work to clear tracks after a January 1977 ice storm that blocked Rigby Yard for a week. **Left**, Maine Central S2 302 spends a Sunday afternoon in September 1974 inside the Waterville roundhouse.

Ronald N. Johnson

Scott Hartley

switchers. The MEC/B&M agreement ended in 1955, and beginning in 1953, MEC's own pine green replaced maroon on road units, and later, new green and yellow schemes evolved on both road units and switchers. At least one S1 also received a black body with yellow nose and cab stripes, a scheme later adopted by Portland Terminal.

What will probably be Maine Central's final paint scheme is the attractive yellow and green trim introduced on 13 EMD GP38's delivered in 1966-67. Subsequent acquisitions and repainted road units also operated in these colors. However, beginning in late 1982, MEC units were repainted in the new charcoal gray color of MEC's new owner Guilford Industries.

Twilight for Maine Central's Alcos came early, beginning with the trade-in of three of the RS2's on GP38's in 1966, leaving just a pair of RS2's to work with the two RS3's on the road's eastern lines. A few of the older Alco switchers were also retired over the following years.

In recent times, MEC has abandoned its allegiance to EMD, starting with the 1975 purchase of 10 U18B's from General Electric. These locomotives allowed the retirement of the RS2's and RS3's, and sent several Geeps into yard service, displacing more Alco switchers.

The end came for Maine Central Alco switchers in 1981 as the railroad began outshopping a group of 15-year old former-Rock Island GE U25B's acquired a year earlier. The GE's, classics in their own right, bumped more Alco switchers, and resulted in the early retirement of the last of the 539-engined units.

The last two Maine Central Alcos, RS11's 801 and 802, are orphans among GP7's, a GP9, GP38's, U18B's, U25B's, and 15 U23B's acquired from the D&H in 1983. The two have been reported retired on several occasions, but they do survive. In late 1983, one of the RS11's was holding down local assignments out of Bangor, while its sister was being cannibalized for parts. Rumors are persistent that both RS11's will be transferred to D&H, a logical move if only in the interest of centralizing parts inventories.

The Portland Terminal Company became a favorite of Alco fans during the 1970's as its all-Alco roster became more and more remarkable among the growing ranks of EMD/GE railroads.

To the amazement and disappointment of those enthusiasts, Maine Central and Boston & Maine EMD

GP7's took over most PT assignments in 1981. Portland Terminal, a Maine Central subsidiary and previously a joint MEC/B&M operation, handles all terminal and switching chores for those two roads in the greater Portland area, including large Rigby Yard in South Portland. The company tried diesels early, purchasing three high-hood Alco HH600's in 1936, and one more in 1938. It followed these acquisitions with more Alcos, S1's and S2's, through the 1940's. Four S4's arrived in late 1950, killing off steam on the PT. Three additional S4's and a single S1, all secondhand, later joined PT's fleet.

Portland Terminal actually did roster one non-Alco diesel, EMD GP7 1081, delivered in 1950. However, the unit spent most of its time working in B&M Boston area commuter service, as part of an MEC/B&M locomotive mileage equalization agreement. It was officially transferred to the Maine Central, along with PT's lone RS11 (see page 31), in 1957.

Portland Terminal's Alco fleet followed the color scheme transitions of parent MEC. The earliest switchers wore plain black, while subsequent units carried the B&M-style black with red nose stripes. Beginning in the sixties, repainted units received the black body with yellow nose and cab end stripes, also worn by at least one MEC Alco. This was the final scheme for PT's fleet.

PT's well-maintained Alcos continued to operate through the seventies, and in view of the loving care the locomotives received from the Rigby roundhouse men, there didn't seem to be any reason why they couldn't run forever.

But parent Maine Central's purchase of new and used locomotives had resulted in a surplus of GP7's, and in 1980 Geeps began appearing on Rigby yard jobs. By late summer 1981, a group of six MEC and four B&M GP7's had silenced the discordant sounds of Alco 539 engines, just as the Alcos had vanquished steam just three decades earlier.

The PT Alco fleet was stored to await disposition. Several units have been sold to shortline and industrial operations (see Chapter 4), and three S's were initially retained for standby service.

A pleasant surprise came in 1983 when S1 1101 was returned to employment at Rigby, chortling contentedly among the green, yellow, and blue EMD replacements. This reprieve, no matter how short, was a happy note on a terminal company that had been all-Alco just three years earlier.

Tom Post

Right, substituting for the usual Baldwin Sharks on D&H's "Slatepicker" job at Castleton, Vt., May 17, 1977, was Bicentennial RS3u 1976. The unit was one of eight RS3's rebuilt by Morrison-Knudsen with 2000-h.p. 251 engines and chopped short hoods. **Above**, Central Vermont's last Alco switcher, S4 8081, brings a way freight past the White River Junction depot in September 1983.

Scott Hartley

Scott Hartley

Until 1981, members of Portland Terminal's all-Alco fleet could be found working throughout the greater Portland area 24 hours a day. **Right**, S4 1057 pulls a cut of cars at the north throat of Rigby Yard past rows of waiting B&M and MEC road diesels in 1977. **Above**, S4 1055 wanders through a remote section of the yard in August 1972. **Below**, S1 1008 is in its final months of service on the PT as it negotiates busy Commercial Street along Portland's waterfront on May 25, 1981.

Maurice B. Quirin

Even as its biggest American connections, the B&M and the NH, were replacing their first diesels with new roadswitchers, the Central Vermont Railway was still assigning chunky 2-8-0's to many local runs. A small number of Alco 1000-h.p. switchers joined the roster in the forties and fifties, and four RS3's held down local freight and passenger chores for a brief period before being sent to Canadian National. CNR provided diesels for the important symbol freights, however, and through the first half of the fifties, handsome green and gold CNR cab units were running all the way to the line's southern terminus at New London, Conn. These were Canadian-built units, virtually identical to American models: General Motors Diesel Ltd. F7's, Canadian Locomotive Company C-Liners and Montreal Locomotive Works FA1's.

Several successive orders for EMD GP9's in 1956-57 spelled the end not only for steam on the CV, but for these interesting Canadian visitors as well.

A number of S2's and S4's remained, and were frequently swapped with sisters from other CNR-owned roads, but mainline freight and remaining passenger

Ronald N. Johnson

activity was usually in the hands of the Geeps.

A surprise motive power reassignment came in 1965 with the arrival of six Alco RS11's from CNR subsidiary Duluth, Winnipeg & Pacific. Three years later, just as most of the engines had been repainted in the then-new black and red scheme with the stylized "wet noodle" CV logo, the RS11's were returned to Minnesota.

The future of Schenectady locomotives on the CV remained bleak for several more years as the number of Alco switchers dwindled to just two S4's. Then in 1977, in a three way CV/GTW/DW&P power swap, CV lost 11 GP9's (and one of the S4's) and received 10 DW&P RS11's, including some of those that had been east a decade earlier.

The Alcos had arrived wearing four different DW&P paint schemes, adding red, orange, and black to the sometimes bland CV lashups. The Central Vermont soon provided more variety by inaugurating its own new scheme, forest green and yellow, a design that spread to the railroad's entire fleet in the following four years.

In 1983, DW&P shipped its five remaining RS11's east, making the CV diesel roster nearly half Alco. In addition to the quintet (of which only 3 were operable), came a boxcar full of 251 parts essential to the continued survival of these engines. One of the RS11's, the 3608, had arrived with a homemade chop nose, and was quickly repainted green, becoming CV's very first low-nose unit. A second RS11 also received CV colors, and the third went to work in DW&P blue.

Despite the added color, Central Vermont operating and mechanical staffs were not particularly pleased with their end of the power swaps. All the Alcos showed signs of age from more than 20 years of heavy tonnage service on the DW&P, and although they were fairly well-maintained, the units suffered failures with annoying regularity. A couple of the first 10 units were deadlined soon after arrival, and the economic situation of the 1980's has allowed three of the units with serious maladies to be stored unserviceable.

For some time, it was apparent that the railway was keeping the Alcos off important runs, and close to the shops at St. Albans, Vermont. Until the arrival of the last five units, RS11's were noticeably absent on Southern Division locals, and on the B&M/CV pool freights. Instead, they were found leading wayfreights in Vermont, and as extra units on St. Albans-Montreal trains. Others were sent to handle local and switcher service on the Grand Trunk in Maine, for which CV is

Scott Hartley

Below, PT S4 1061 gets its sanders filled before being put to bed at the Rigby enginehouse in March 1981. **Above**, in happier times, S1 1007 and S2 1052 are seen resting at Rigby in August 1977.

Ronald N. Johnson

Both photos, Gary Knapp

The transfer of 15 Duluth, Winnipeg & Pacific RS11's to Central Vermont has resulted in the appearance of the notch-nosed Alcos on just about every CV train assignment. **Above**, six RS11's provide a spectacular show as they bring northbound 447 across the White River near Royalton, Vt., Aug. 13, 1983. In late 1983, four-, five- and even six-unit sets of Alcos were regularly assigned to this run. **Left**, father and son wave to crews on caboose and helpers as two RS11's lean their muscle into train 444's 11,000 tons at Duxbury, Vt., on a summer 1982 evening.

responsible for providing motive power. Beginning in 1983, however, with five less Geeps on the roster, the RS11's are common all over the Central Vermont. A frequent treat for Alco fans has been the sight of four, five, and even six of the notch-nose hoods struggling to move 100 cars of the St. Albans-White River Junction freight uphill to the top of the ruling grade at Roxbury.

One Central Vermont RS11 appears different from its sisters, with boxy louvered covers over its ventilation ducts. Unit 3609 is actually the second RS11 to carry that number, the first engine having been wrecked on the Boston & Maine in 1979. CV acquired a retired RS11 from the Norfolk & Western and rebuilt it, utilizing the healthy mechanical parts from the original 3609. One advantage with the new unit is it has dual engineer controls, for operation in either direction. As a result, the engine initially spent quite a bit of its time in fairly high-speed service, on CV's hotshot piggyback train, the *Rocket*.

One other locomotive on CV's roster is important to consider in this view of the Alco in twilight. The road's last Alco switcher, S4 8081, has in recent years spent some time at White River Junction and New London, but it usually considers Italy Yard in St. Albans as home. A relatively young S4, built in 1955, it has spent its entire life on its home road, is well maintained, and is likely to be the last active Central Vermont Alco.

The small town of East Alburg, Vt., on the Canadian border, 15.6 miles north of St. Albans, is CV's actual connection with parent Canadian National. No interchange is handled there, and both CNR and CV crews and locomotives have traditionally shared assignments between Montreal and St. Albans. In the last few years as CV's power has grown older and consequently less reliable, Canadian National engines have predominated on trains north of St. Albans. Montreal Locomotive Works wide-cab M420R's are the usual locomotives on these runs, with GP38-2's and CV units also appearing occasionally. As Central Vermont's motive power situation grew tighter in the 1980's, the MLW's began running south to White River Junction, and occasionally beyond. Canadian National 2500-2579 are by far the newest Alco-type diesels operating in New England, constructed by MLW between 1973 and 1976. (In addition, 10 similar HR412's, built by MLW successor Bombardier in 1980, power Central Vermont trains from time to time.)

Central Vermont's newest diesel is an EMD SW1200 built in 1960. Obviously, the road's motive power ros-

Above, CV's first—and so far only—low-nose unit is RS11 3608, shown cresting the grade at Roxbury, Vt., with train 447 in June 1983. **Left,** a pair of Canadian National M420's leads four RS11's and a GP9 as they arrive in St. Albans, Vt., with a very late train 444, July 5, 1978. The big MLW's usually run as far south as this point, but occasionally continue beyond. Note the variety of paint schemes on the Alcos and Geep.

Ronald N. Johnson

ter is old and tired, and will need replacing in the next couple of years. How this will be accomplished is only subject for speculation, but the Central Vermont remains a major attraction for Alco fans in the mid-1980's.

The Delaware & Hudson Railway no longer operates trains in New England. The company has recently given up its marginal Washington and Rutland branches, which both ran for a few miles in the state of Vermont. However, during the preceding years, just about every type of unit from D&H's varied Alco stable could be found on the branches' few trains.

In earlier days, the railroad's 1000 h.p. Alco switchers and RS2 and RS3 roadswitchers were common sights. Later, RS11's and RS36's appeared as well. D&H's frequent motive power shortages during the seventies brought borrowed Alcos on the line, including those from Canadian Pacific, United Railway Supply, and dealer-owned ex-Long Island units. Eight D&H RS3's were upgraded and chop-nosed by Morrison-Knudsen, and former-Lehigh Valley and Lehigh & Hudson River C420's joined the D&H roster, all in the late seventies.

Railfans flocked to the area from 1975 through 1977, when the road's two former-Monongahela, ex-New York Central Baldwin "Sharknose" RF16's held down the regularly-assigned jobs on both branches out of Whitehall, N.Y., the daytime "Slatepicker" down the Washington Branch to Greenwich Junction (connection with D&H subsidiary Greenwich & Johnsonville), and the weeknight "Hill Freight" to the VTR/GMRC connections at Rutland. Despite this seemingly excellent power utilization, the Baldwins suffered from frequent illnesses and visiting fans at that time were often disappointed to find an Alco covering the day's local freight.

Remarkably, D&H's ever-popular PA's even made a couple of runs over the spindly rails of the branches in 1977, after being bumped from Amtrak's *Adirondack* and prior to being leased to the MBTA for Boston commuter service.

The railway's status as an operating museum ended with the resignation of president C. Bruce Sterzing in 1977. Nevertheless, the locomotives of Schenectady were still well represented on the roster, and Alcos could be found more often than not powering the decreasing number of as-needed trains on the Vermont branches.

Much of the Washington Branch was embargoed in the late seventies, and finally abandoned by the D&H in 1981. The southern end of the branch, all in New York, as well as the 17-mile former-Greenwich & Johnsonville, are now operated by the new Batten Kill Railroad with its ex-G&J RS3. The northern portion of the line may also see service again, likely under the auspices of the State of Vermont. In 1983, the D&H pulled out of the remainder of its Vermont lines, the Whitehall to Rutland branch. The Vermont Railway now operates the line.

Thus, despite the end of the D&H service, it appears that the new operators of this trackage will continue the tradition and run their own Alco diesels over these scenic branches.

Fortunately for Alco fans, D&H diesels, including those built at Schenectady, have continued to be visible in New England on B&M pool freights. These operations are discussed above.

37

Garry Knapp

A pair of CV RS11's move a southbound way freight through Middlesex, Vt., in 1982, with granite flats in the train's consist.

Scott Hartley

Scott Hartley

Three of the 3600's await duty at the St. Albans roundhouse in September 1981.

Scott Hartley

Below left, CV's second 3609 is a former-N&W RS11, and is unlike its ex-DW&P sisters in that it has dual engineer controls, which allows the engine to operate with either end leading, instead of long-hood forward like most other CV roadswitchers. As a result, 3609 spent its first couple years on the railroad leading the hotshot *Rocket* piggybacker. It is shown leaving Palmer, Mass., during a summer downpour in 1981. **Left**, CV S4 8081 is shown in black-and-red colors at St. Albans in 1979. **Below**, the 8081 is in green and working a ballast train at Windsor, Vt., Sept. 2, 1981.

Scott Hartley

Bangor & Aroostook's only Alco, MLW S3 20, is shown working at Madawaska, Me., April 7, 1973, during its brief stay on the railroad. **Left**, Delaware & Hudson C420 414 is still wearing the red of former owner Lehigh Valley as it handles the "Slatepicker," at Rupert, Vt., March 1, 1977. **Below**, just one week later, the same train is shown at West Pawlet, Vt., behind a leased CP Rail RS3.

The Bangor & Aroostook deserves a brief mention in this volume. Despite its dependence on the American Locomotive Company in the days of steam, BAR (or B&A, as it is known to the locals) has relied almost entirely on EMD diesels. It is true that the railroad borrowed New Haven RS2's and DL109's to combat traffic upswings and power shortages of the 1950's, but the road's diesel roster remained exclusively General Motors. Or at least it did until 1972, when BAR picked up a 65-ton GE and an ex-Canadian National MLW S3 from a paper company. The Alco carried its previous owner's yellow and blue colors, with spartan BAR stencilling, and even worked for a while in switching and local service before being placed in storage, and subsequently resold. The BAR remains as the only major New England line that Alco salesmen couldn't persuade.

CP Rail C424 4241 leads two RS18's into the United States at Richford, Vt., Jan. 27, 1983. As the three MLW's are passing the large Webster feed facility, the train's caboose is still across the border in Canada.

Paul Lambert

3/Visitors from the north

In the 1980's, America's neighbor to the north is the Promised Land for Alco fans.

In Canada, Alco licensee Montreal Locomotive Works stayed close to competitor General Motors Diesel in tallies of units built. And even when Alco quit in 1969, MLW continued to build Alco's Century line, and later its own "M"-style hoods. Though GMD has far outsold MLW and its corporate successor, Bombardier, Ltd., in recent years, there are still lots of Alco-design diesels in the Dominion.

Fortunately for New Englanders, Canada's two transcontinental rail systems, Canadian National and CP Rail, both concentrate their MLW fleets in the eastern regions of the vast nation. As a result, Alcos dominate CN and CP lines in Vermont, New Hampshire and Maine.

Until the late 1940's, CPR was still virtually an all-steam railroad. The company had been assembling a sizeable fleet of S2 switchers built by Alco at Schenectady, and CPR's Vancouver Island lines were dieselized with Baldwin/Canadian Locomotive Company units in late 1948, but steam still reigned supreme on the high iron.

However, the writing was already on the wall for the ultimate future of steam, and CPR chose its lines in Vermont to be an experimental proving ground for the new internal combustion invaders. In a nine-month period in 1949, 23 diesel units arrived to replace steam on the Montreal-Newport-St. Johnsbury-Wells River route. The breakdown was 8 FA1's, 4 FB1's, 5 RS2's and 3 S2's, all built by Alco at Schenectady. All were purchased from the U.S. builder to avoid paying import duties for the units intended for use south of the border; further, MLW had only begun building diesels a year earlier and was not yet equipped to manufacture road units. Similarly, three E8's were delivered to CP lines in Vermont from Electro-Motive at La Grange, Ill., as EMD's Canadian counterpart, General Motors Diesel, would not open its London, Ont., plant for another year.

It is only speculative to wonder why EMD E's got the nod over Alco's competitive PA. Perhaps it was because the three EMD's would be used in joint CPR/B&M Montreal-Boston service, where the American road was already operating a fleet of E7's. As it was, no PA was delivered to any Canadian road, and CPR "Vermont E8's" 1800-1802 remained the only E's in the Dominion.

The new diesels proved successful coping with the undulating profiles of the Vermont lines, and it was inevitable that shiny new maroon-and-gray MLW FA and GMD F diesels were soon pushing aside steam across CPR's transcontinental system.

New FA's and FB's joined the original 12 on Vermont road jobs and as more and more diesels arrived on the CPR, the road concentrated its MLW fleet in the eastern portion of its system. As roadswitchers came in favor over cab units, successive generations of MLW RS3's, RS10's and RS18's began appearing in Vermont. However, the original five RS2's and three S2's continued to reside in the Green Mountain State, holding down yard and way-freight duties.

By the late 1960's, when CPR's classic maroon colors

began to give way to the new CP Rail "Action Red" scheme, MLW roadswitchers were in charge of virtually all Vermont trains, with FA's and GMD FP7's making rare appearances.

In the mid-1970's, as CP Rail retired its 244-engined units, MLW C424's began to appear in their place. For a brief period CP's C630, M630 and M636 types were showing up as far south as St. Johnsbury, but after a couple of minor yard derailments, the big six-axle units were deemed too heavy for the line.

Canadian Pacific began a long-range program to rebuild many of its first-generation GMD and MLW diesels in 1979, and soon after, newly chopnosed RS18's began to run in Vermont. Throughout all of these motive-power advances, the original five RS2's and three S2's continued to brighten the Vermont countryside. All had been built without m.u. capability, which kept them out of heavier through freight service, and this feature no doubt contributed to their longevity.

But like all good things, this attraction had to end. CP Rail had ceased heavy overhauls on its 244-engined MLW's (and Alcos) in 1979, and it was only a matter of time before the elderly RS2's would be set aside. Remarkably, all five RS2's were still in daily service in June 1983 when they were replaced by rebuilt RS18's. The three S2's had been placed in storage a year earlier.

In addition to a couple of branches that just barely poke into Vermont and Maine, CP Rail's other New England entry is its International of Maine Division, which cuts some 200 miles across the northern half of that state as part of the railway's Montreal-St. John, N.B., route. Unlike the Vermont lines, this division was dieselized at a gradual rate. Diesels did not appear there until 1954, and new diesels supplanted steam over a period of years. The last coal-burning locomotives actually survived into 1960, with little 4-6-2's on a Brownville Jct., Me.-Megantic, Que., mixed-train assignment that became a favorite target for photographers in its final years.

Maine trains ran with the same MLW-dominated power as that of other eastern CPR runs: first FA's, then RS3's, RS10's and RS18's. Canadian-built engines were often joined by a couple of the Vermont RS2 and S2 types on local and switching assignments. A few Canadian-only MLW switcher models such as S10's, S11's and RS23's have worked Maine jobs as well.

Just as in Vermont, as older 244 power was retired, newer MLW's were assigned to the International route. By the early 1980's, regular road power on the Maine

Both photos, Scott Hartley

Canadian Pacific's classic maroon-and-gray colors graced Vermont rails through the 1970's, although the new red CP Rail scheme had become prevalent by the middle of the decade. **Above**, FPA2 4095 leads three RS10's and a leased B&M RS3 upgrade at Barton, Vt., in 1969. **Right**, Alco-built S2 7098 works St. Johnsbury yard in July 1971.

Alco and MLW diesels have always been the usual power on CP's Vermont lines. RS2 8400 was already 30 years old but still going strong as it worked near Richford in 1979.

Three photos, Scott Hartley

Below, American-built S2 7096 compares profiles with Canadian C424 4245 at Newport in May 1979. **Above**, RS2 8403 was in its final days of active duty in June 1983 as it shared the Newport enginehouse tracks with rebuilt RS18's.

42

Both photos, Ronald N. Johnson

Alco power is also a regular feature on CP Rail's International of Maine Division. At **right**, a single 244-engined RS3 works with four 251-powered RS18's on a St. John, N.B.-Montreal, Que., container train at Brownville Junction, Me., in 1976. Six-motor MLW's frequent the Maine route as well. **Above**, three massive M636's await a nighttime call at Brownville Junction yard in September 1981.

line was mixes of four- and six-axle Century types built by MLW, as well as standard and rebuilt RS18's. Local work was handled by MLW switchers and road-switchers.

In the middle of the 1980's, CP Rail's Vermont and Maine routes offer the best opportunities for viewing big-time Alco action in New England. Six-unit sets of bright red 251-engined hoods, struggling up Vance Hill out of Newport, Vt., or winding through rugged timberland near Jackman, Me., make for some very exciting train-watching.

VIA Rail Canada, the Dominion's rail passenger corporation, made a surprise contribution to northern New England Alco fans in the late 1970's. Maine's last passenger train had been CP Rail's *Atlantic Limited*, an overnight Montreal-St. John run which passed through the Pine Tree State under the cover of darkness.

In earlier years, CPR had assigned steam generator-equipped MLW FPA2's to the run, but by the early 1970's, the usual power had been one of the two remaining EMD E8's or a GMD FP7. VIA took over the train in 1978 and a year later lengthened its run to Halifax; as a result, the usual consist of about five cars expanded to more than a dozen. The rare E8's were reassigned, but their replacements were equally acceptable: More often than not, a lashup of VIA's former-CNR FPA4's led the new *Atlantic*. Thus, Alco-design cab units actually made a brief resurgence in New England before the politically-inspired cancellation of the popular train in November 1981.

In addition to its ownership of the Central Vermont, the Dominion's government-controlled transcontinental, Canadian National, itself operates in three New England states.

CN's Berlin Subdivision, also known as the Grand Trunk Railway, begins at Island Pond, Vt., and runs through New Hampshire to Portland, Me. The Grand Trunk label dates back to the line's beginnings as part of an ambitious cross-Canada transcontinental, originating from the deep-water harbor of Portland. St. John and Halifax long ago eclipsed Portland in importance as seaport towns, but the Grand Trunk nevertheless continues to provide an important link in CN's freight route from Maine to Montreal and on to Midwestern U.S. Although GT has been just another subdivision of its huge parent system, the line has displayed more than a little independence over the years. Until recently, locomotives and rolling stock have carried GT lettering.

Grand Trunk and Canadian National steam held down assignments on this line through the early 1950's. CNR road diesels began to show up on varnish and symbol freights at that time. It was not until 1954 that GT's first diesels, a pair of Alco RS3's, arrived on the property. The two usually handled the Portland-Gorham (N.H.) way freights until they were transferred, first to Central Vermont, then to CNR, in 1957. A Grand Trunk-lettered Alco S4 was also purchased in 1956, but it spent very little time on its assigned road.

Text continued on page 46

Scott Hartley

Mike Schafer

Sadly, most of the Alcos and MLW's shown on this page are now retired. At **left**, RS2 8404 reaches the top of the southbound grade at Summit, Vt., on a rainy Aug. 24, 1979. **Above**, an MLW RS3 is the lead unit on a joint CP-B&M runthrough from Newport, Vt., that has just arrived St. Johnsbury, Vt., in July 1974. **Below**, S2 7096 works St. Johnsbury yard in the fall of 1976 under the watchful eye of a Maine Central GP7.

Mike Schafer

Scott Hartley

Vermont remains an attraction with Alco-watchers, with frequent surprises such as, at **left**, a pair of rare MLW RS23's leading two RS18's northbound at Richford in September 1983. Action of CP Rail's International of Maine Division has nothing to apologize for either. **Below left**, three FP4's and a CP RS10 are on the point of the *Atlantic* as the popular train makes its predawn stop at Brownville Junction on Dec. 18, 1979. **Below**, a big M636 and two C424's roll a westbound freight through Mattawamkeag in August 1983.

D. D. Perry

Pete Coulombe, collection of Ronald N. Johnson

Steam locomotive fires were dumped for good in the late 1950's because of the 1956-57 delivery of 16 EMD GP9's. These Geeps, which were frequently exchanged for members of CV's almost identical fleet, were the rule on most GT local trains for two decades. Through freights were powered by the GT/CV Geeps, as well as locomotives from other CN family roads, including Duluth, Winnipeg & Pacific RS11's and CN RS18's. Passenger service, which was terminated in the 1960's, usually rated a steam-equipped GP9 or RS18, but CN flat-nose FPA's also visited the Grand Trunk.

In the early sixties, all of GT's locomotives were officially transferred to CV ownership, and CV was contracted to provide and maintain units for GT use. Despite this arrangement, Grand Trunk's Geeps continued to carry GT insignias, right up through the "wet noodle" logo era.

Since the mid-1970's, the usual road power on the daily Montreal-Portland symbol freight has been three or four MLW 251-engined Canadian wide-cab M420R's. Occasionally a GMD GP38-2 will show up, but most days solid lashups of Alco-design engines will put on a fine show through the beautiful forests of northern New Hampshire and Vermont.

In the late 1970's, CV and GT GP9's were being transferred to sister road Grand Trunk Western, and were replaced by DW&P RS11's. Since then, these Alcos have held down most GT way-freight and switching assignments.

The few remaining GT Geeps have been repainted in CV's new green color scheme, complete with CV lettering. As of the mid-1980's, only some cabooses and MofW cars still carry Grand Trunk reporting marks, but it is encouraging to Alco fans that practically every chore on the railroad is capably handled by 251-powered locomotives.

Ninety-six-hundred MLW horsepower teams up to move westbound tonnage over CP Rail's Onawa, Me., trestle in February 1976.

Ronald N. Johnson

Both photos, Ronald N. Johnson

Maine railroading is often a study in contrasts. **Above**, CP Rail C424's move a St. John (N.B.)-bound container train across the unusual round-top steel trestle at Mattawamkeag. However, CP also operates several light-density branches into the Pine Tree State from New Brunswick. At **left**, RS23 8022 enters the weedy yard at Houlton with one hopper car of grain on Sept. 15, 1980. The once-a-week way freight will stop at the dilapidated depot so that U.S. Customs officials may clear the car.

In the mid-1980's, Canadian Pacific's original Schenectady diesels may be retired, but Alco action still abounds in Vermont, as evidenced by these views photographed during the summer of 1983. **Right**, a quartet of C424's rolls past a working dairy farm at Newport Center. **Below**, a remarkable consist of seven RS18's moves train 937 north through Newport Center.

Three photos, Scott Hartley

Four RS18's crest the Connecticut/St. Lawrence divide at Summit.

Both photos, Ronald N. Johnson

Canadian National's fleets of MLW M420R's and Bombardier HR412's are today's regular power on the Grand Trunk through Maine, New Hampshire and Vermont. **At right**, a trio of new M420's works through Shelburne, N.H., in 1975. **Above**, Portland-Montreal freight 393 departs GT's Portland waterfront yard March 7, 1978.

Garland McKee

Regular switching and way-freight power on the Grand Trunk in the 1980's is from CV's RS11 fleet. Here, CV 3612 pumps out a cloud on an otherwise clear New England day while working Grand Trunk local 796 at Island Pond, Vt., Sept. 15, 1981.

49

Gary Knapp

Despite the use of Central Vermont and Canadian National diesels, there are still a few traces to remind train-watchers of the Grand Trunk heritage of CN's Montreal-Portland line. **Right**, the office building at Portland proudly proclaims "Grand Trunk Railway" in November 1981 as a CV RS11 works the local switching assignment. **Above right**, CV RS11 3605 treads carefully along busy Commercial Street in Portland on its way back to the GT yard after interchanging with the Portland Terminal in June 1981. **Above**, four CN M420R's make quite a show as they work through Vermont's Northeast Kingdom in 1982.

Ronald N. Johnson

Ronald N. Johnson

Tom Nelligan

Ronald N. Johnson

Below right, three CN M420's struggle for traction as they move Grand Trunk train 393 out of Berlin, N.H., in September 1979. **Above**, a trio of brand new wide-cabs rolls along the Androscoggin River near Shelburne, N.H., March 9, 1975. **Above right**, a Central Vermont GP9 adds its tractive effort to the usual M420's as train 393 crosses a stream near Pownal, Me., in July 1979.

Tom Nelligan

Former Southern Railway RS3 1601 is shown in its one-of-a-kind Providence & Worcester paint scheme at Plainfield, Conn., in 1976.
Scott Hartley

4/Short lines and newcomers

The survival of existing short lines and the birth and development of new railroads in New England have been responsible for the continued life of many of the region's Alcos. Simply stated, second-hand EMD Geeps and yard units are more popular than used Alcos, and applying the laws of supply and demand, a pre-owned RS3 costs a lot less than a GP7 of comparative age. As a rule, shortline railroads are seldom wealthy; thus it's cheaper to acquire a fleet of old Alcos. And that's what has happened on many New England lines.

Successful short lines (e.g., Vermont Railway, Providence & Worcester) have quickly turned to EMD when the profits started rolling in. But most small railroads can only wish they were so lucky, while their elderly Alcos are nursed, cajoled and forced to keep rolling. Some are now 40 years old, but they do keep rolling.

The big success story in New England railroading in recent years has been the Providence & Worcester. Breaking free of 85 years of New Haven and Penn Central control in 1973, P&W has grown from a 50-mile line connecting its namesake cities to a sprawling 371-mile rail system, plus diversified businesses, through Massachusetts, Rhode Island and Connecticut. It has taken over smaller short lines, picked up unwanted former-NH branches from Conrail, wrested ownership of other more-profitable lines away from CR, and acquired freight trackage rights over much of Amtrak's Shore Line route.

As the P&W has grown, so has the size and variety of its locomotive roster. Operations were begun in 1973 with six leased Delaware & Hudson RS3's, all but one of which wore P&W's attractive orange-chocolate-white colors.

When P&W went shopping for its own diesels, the two big locomotive builders were understandably reluctant to extend credit to the maverick corporation. The skepticism of EMD and GE had its rewards for locomotive fans; P&W didn't bother returning to the two American manufacturers, but instead went north of the border to Canada's Montreal Locomotive Works. The firm was eager to penetrate the U.S. market, and in 1974 and 1975 delivered five of its M420R freight locomotives to the P&W.

The tall Canadians, carrying 2000-h.p. model 251 engines and featuring Canadian National-style crew safety cowl cabs, introduced a parallelogram-shaped scheme of the P&W colors. As the new M420's arrived, the leased RS3's were returned to D&H. However, in 1976, P&W needed additional power to operate its growing system and purchased a pair of former-Southern Railway RS3's. The newcomers operated in SR black for some time until being repainted in yet two new variations of P&W colors. An additional Alco, Maine Central RS2 553, soon arrived at the South Worcester shops to provide parts for the two RS3's. The elderly Alco was actually operable, though, and it held down a variety of P&W switching and work train assignments, still wearing MEC green, until its two younger sisters began to require transplants.

Along with P&W's growth and success came recognition by locomotive builders of P&W's financial sta-

52

Above, P&W's first scheme was applied to five leased D&H RS3's. Two are shown at South Worcester in May 1973. The large white areas proved to be difficult to keep clean, and the railroad's next locomotives, five MLW M420R's, introduced a new arrangement of orange, brown and white, as shown on 2002 and 2004, **below right**. P&W's latest scheme was introduced in 1982, and is seen on M420 2001 powering a passenger extra at Northbridge, Mass., May 14, 1983, **right**.

All photos, Scott Hartley

bility, and the railroad has bought American since 1976. General Electric provided a U18B and a B23-7, and Electro-Motive delivered four GP38-2's between 1980 and 1982. Purchase of a pair of ex-CR, ex-Pennsy GP9's in 1982 allowed the retirement of P&W's two RS3's, which were sold for parts supplies to Vermont's Lamoille Valley Railroad.

It's safe to assume that P&W's future locomotive needs will be met by American builders, and that the one-time reign of Alco diesels is gone forever. The railroad's five M420R's (still the only MLW engines sold new to a U.S. railroad) continue to thrive with their GE and EMD companions, however, and should be with us for some time to come.

The government of the State of Vermont has been at least partially responsible for the survival of 244- and 539-engined diesels in several regions of the Green Mountain State. Alcos have provided the backbone of the rosters of the several private operators of state-owned trackage since Vermont entered the railroad

Left, newly delivered M420R's 2004 and 2003 cross the Blackstone River at Valley Falls, R.I., June 15, 1975. **Above**, an often unremarked P&W Alco was RS2 1501, formerly Maine Central 553, purchased as a parts supply but used as a switcher and work train engine for a lengthy period before being placed in storage.

Ronald N. Johnson

Scott Hartley

Ex-Southern 1602 and Canadian-built 2001 spend idle moments together at South Worcester, Mass., in April 1980.

Scott Hartley

business more than two decades ago.

It all began with the shutdown of the Rutland Railroad in 1961. Faced with the bleak prospect of no rail service through large sections of Vermont, the state government stepped in and purchased Rutland's tracks from Burlington south through Rutland to Bennington, as well as the Rutland-Bellows Falls line. Operations for both were contracted out to private companies, with the Vermont Railway commencing service between Burlington and Bennington in 1964, and the Green Mountain Railroad starting operations from Rutland to Bellows Falls the following year.

Much more recently, the state has expanded its involvement in railroading with the 1973 purchase of the unlucky St. Johnsbury & Lamoille County. The StJ&LC has been in the hands of a multitude of operators under various names, both before and after the state purchase, but currently survives as the all-Alco Lamoille Valley Railroad. And in 1980, Vermont acquired the little Montpelier & Barre, which connects those two cities and their surrounding granite quarries. This line is now managed locally and known as the Washington County Railroad.

The Rutland Railroad had dieselized with a fleet of 9 RS3's and 6 RS1's, and with the exception of a single GE 70 tonner, the road remained all-Alco until its

Jack Armstrong

Vermont Railway RS3 605 on the freight from Rutland and Boston & Maine GP9 1702 powering the local over from Mechanicville, N.Y., meet at North Bennington, Vt., Oct. 14, 1981. Today, VTR operates the B&M branch from North Bennington to Hoosic Junction, N.Y., and the two roads interchange there.

Scott Hartley

Scott Hartley

Left, S4 6 hustles down the VTR main line at Center Rutland, returning to Rutland with the Clarendon & Pittsford job, July 21, 1977. **Above**, the C&P crew puts RS3 603 away at Rutland after a long week, on Friday, May 23, 1980.

Above, Vermont Railway S4 No. 6, a former Chesapeake & Ohio unit, was acquired to operate on VTR subsidiary Clarendon & Pittsford. It is shown at Florence, Vt., Nov. 1, 1977. **Left**, by the early 1980's, VTR's Alco fleet was down to just three RS3's. A pair of them is shown inside the Burlington roundhouse July 25, 1983.

Jack Armstrong

Scott Hartley

abandonment. Most of this comparatively young roster quickly found new owners, but a few of these Alcos stayed close to home.

The Vermont Railway began its operations with three former Rutland RS1's, as well as a couple of GE 44-tonners and an ex-DL&W EMD SW1. Another RS1, from the Soo Line, replaced the diminutive GE's before VTR made its first new locomotive purchase of an EMD SW1500, in 1966. Later acquisitions were of a variety of second-hand Alco RS3's. All were painted in Vermont's attractive red-and-white color scheme.

As business continued to improve, the early smaller power, including the RS1's, were sold. The railroad entered the big time in the 1970's with the purchase of two EMD GP38-2's. VTR also picked up an ex-C&O S4 to operate on the Clarendon & Pittsford, a 20-mile connecting short line the road had taken over in 1972. The S was sold in 1980. VTR became even more EMD-dominated a year later when it picked up a Conrail GP9. The railroad has also taken over operations of the B&M branch from North Bennington, Vt., to Hoosic Junction, N.Y., and D&H's Whitehall, N.Y.-Rutland line in recent years, making the additional locomotives necessary.

By the end of 1983, Vermont Railway's last two RS3's could be found in daily service, usually as the Burlington switcher and on the C&P job out of Rutland, but the Alcos were for sale if the right buyer came along. At the same time, the road was buying a GP18 and an SW1500 from the Toledo, Peoria & Western and was considering the purchase of a Burlington Northern GP9 as well. Clearly these new EMD's bear bad tidings for the pair of RS3's.

An additional 50 miles of Rutland was revived as a result of New England businessman F. Nelson Blount's search for a rail line to operate his growing collection of steam locomotives. When Blount agreed to operate the Rutland-Bellows Falls line, his main objective had been to find a location for a steam museum and trackage to run steam-powered passenger trains. As part of the lease agreement, however, Blount's Green Mountain Railroad Corporation would also handle freight service on the newly acquired line.

Initially, GMRC planned to run all of its trains behind steam power, but immediately prior to inauguration of service in April 1965, Rutland RS1 405 was purchased to handle freight operations.

Blount had previously acquired Boston & Maine's yard and roundhouse at North Walpole, N.H., just across the Connecticut River from Bellows Falls, as an operational and maintenance base for his steam collection, and the new freight service soon began running out of this facility. A pair of D&H S4's (plus an S2 for parts) joined GMRC's roster in the late sixties. All engines were painted in the old Rutland eye-pleasing green-and-yellow colors.

In the first years, GMRC handled Bellows Falls-Rutland freight operations, as well as Steamtown's steam passenger trains between the museum at Riverside and Chester. Following Blount's untimely death in 1967, Green Mountain and Steamtown emerged from probate as separate entities, and by 1971 the last of GMRC's steam fleet had been transferred to Steamtown ownership.

Following the separation, GMRC retained the North Walpole facilities, and operated its freight trains from there. Steamtown locomotives were maintained at Riverside, and run by Steamtown crews over leased

56

Mike Schafer

Green Mountain not only took over operations on 50 miles of abandoned Rutland trackage, but adopted Rutland's attractive green-and-yellow paint scheme as well. **Above**, a pair of RS1's crosses the Connecticut River from North Walpole, N.H., into Bellow Falls, Vt., with the local freight to Rutland in June 1981. **Right**, S4 303 and RS1 405 move upgrade along the Williams River at Gassetts, June 28, 1972.

Jack Armstrong

Mike Schafer

Left, RS1 401 (ex-Illinois Central Gulf, GM&O, Illinois Terminal) passes a typical Vermont townscape at Bartonsville in June 1981. **Below**, GMR's two ex-D&H S4's work at North Walpole, N.H., in July 1971.

Scott Hartley

57

Right, the 405 is shown with the weekday North Walpole-Rutland local freight, Feb. 16, 1972, at Gassetts, Vt. **Above**, S4 303 is seen with a plow extra later the same day.

Both photos, Scott Hartley

GMRC trackage rights. Steamtown plans to move its entire museum and train operations to the Scranton, Pa., area in 1984, so meets between ex-CPR 4-6-2's and green Alco diesels may be over.

In the mid-1970's GMRC expanded its Alco fleet when it got a good deal on a pair of former-GM&O, ex-IT RS1's, purchased from the Illinois Central Gulf. The two red Alcos languished for some time until the first, carrying Green Mountain number 401, emerged in green-and-yellow in 1979. The second Midwestern emigrant finally went to work in late 1983.

The Green Mountain also expanded its operations in the late 1970's when it began switching B&M's yard at Keene, N.H. In 1982, the GMRC took over the entire Brattleboro, Vt.-Keene line, but this operation was shortlived and was abandoned by fall 1983.

With three RS1's more than sufficient to handle its operating needs, GMRC planned to store and/or sell the two S4's. And also in late 1983, the railroad tested a Maine Central RS11 for a week to determine the operating efficiencies that could be derived from operating larger motive power.

In the past several years, the Green Mountain has suffered plant closures of on-line customers as well as major track damage caused by northern New England weather. But despite these setbacks, the small line has hung on. The GMRC's Alcos are kept healthy and clean, and with luck, will continue to brighten the southern Vermont countryside for several more years.

A more recent addition to the Vermont state government's railroad system is the trackage of the St. Johnsbury & Lamoille County. When the first construction of the StJ&LC began in the 1860's, plans called for the line to be an essential link in a rail system connecting the Atlantic Ocean at Portland, Me., with the Great Lakes and Chicago. Instead, when the flurry of railroad building of the late nineteenth century ended, the "St. J" found itself as just another short line, with most through traffic traveling over parallel systems.

The 96-mile line survived through the years, however, with ownership passing from the B&M to local interests and on to assorted shortline operators. What didn't change was the generally sorry state of the railroad's trackage and the decrepit locomotives that powered its trains.

The StJ&LC became of interest to Alco enthusiasts when the line was purchased by shortline entrepreneur Samuel M. Pinsly in 1967. Actually, many fans at the time were disappointed when second-hand Alco RS3's and EMD GP9's replaced the multi-unit lashups of the road's tired GE 70-tonners, but for once the management of the never-do-well line seemed to be making genuine attempts to modernize the St. J.

The newly arrived Geeps and RS3's brought with them the Pinsly system's attractive color scheme of red, black and yellow. The big engines could be seen hauling heavier trains on rebuilt track as the new owners attempted to attract through traffic back to the railroad.

The two former-New York Central GP9's were to be Pinsly's only EMD's. But over the years of his ownership of the StJ&LC, he brought five RS3's onto the property: a pair from the Lehigh & Hudson River, and one each from the Reading, Great Northern and D&H.

By the early 1970's, Pinsly had come to realize his railroad just was not going to be a big money-maker. Despite his sincere efforts, the railroad continued to lose money while derailments became more frequent. Pinsly proposed abandonment, and also offered the line for sale to the state.

After prolonged negotiations, the state did purchase

Ronald N. Johnson

Above, in the days of Pinsly ownership, Montpelier & Barre S1 29 brings granite past the Barre depot, Feb. 6, 1976. Today's Washington County operates with M&B's two former-B&M S1's. **Left**, WC 25 stops at the Central Vermont freight office at Montpelier Junction to pick up waybills on Sept. 2, 1981.

Below, the 25 shows off freshly painted silver trucks. **Below left**, an S1 leaves the CV interchange with New Jersey Transit commuter car shells en route to Bombardier's Barre assembly plant in August 1982.

Scott Hartley

Tom Nelligan   Scott Hartley

Scott Hartley

Below, an attractive but short lived scheme was carried on Wolfeboro's RS3 101, shown with a passenger special running along Lake Winnisquam, N.H., Aug. 2, 1976. **Right**, new Pinsly short line Pioneer Valley has brought Alcos to former-NH trackage in western Massachusetts. Former-Frankfort & Cincinnati (nee-C&O) S2 106 meets 1939 EMC SW1 at Westfield, Oct. 10, 1983. **Above**, Grafton & Upton S4 1001 is seen working at Hopedale, Mass., in May 1976.

Scott Hartley

Ronald N. Johnson

the St. J., in early 1973, although Pinsly continued to operate it for its new owners until late summer of that year.

A new corporation comprised of northern Vermont businessmen was awarded the contract to operate the St. J. The line was run as the Lamoille County Railroad until the new management restored the StJ&LC roadname six months later. This reincarnation of the St. J utilized a couple of Pinsly's leftover RS3's, as well as two ex-Reading GP7's painted in an unattractive Bicentennial paint scheme.

The local businessmen didn't fare much better with the railroad, and after financial losses and an employee strike, the state awarded the St. J contract to yet another operator, international construction company Morrison-Knudsen. M-K was probably more interested in being awarded a large contract for the state- and federally-funded rebuilding of the StJ&LC's track, but nevertheless the company enthusiastically took over the dilapidated railroad, which it renamed the Vermont Northern.

VN brought in the most unlikely motive power to operate on a line where speed limits rarely exceeded 8 miles per hour. Three ex-Long Island high-nose Alco C420's, still painted in LIRR blue-and-yellow, went to work between St. Johnsbury and Swanton, with little

Mike Schafer

Bruce P. Curry

Mike Schafer

Many colors have been worn by the plethora of Alcos that have run on the old St. Johnsbury & Lamoille County. **Above**, "St.J" RS3 204 is still in Pinsly red as it rolls westward toward Swanton, Vt., in July 1974. **Above right**, Vermont Northern owner Morrison-Knudsen introduced its yellow-and-black scheme on one of its three ex-Long Island C420's just a short time before it quit operating the line at the end of 1977; No. 204 is at Morrisville shops, Dec. 27, 1977. Bright yellow is the color of current St.J operator Lamoille Valley. Chopnose RS3's are seen at East Highgate, **right**, and Sheldon Junction, **below**, in May 1981.

Mike Schafer

Bruce P. Curry

Jack Armstrong

Above left, St. Johnsbury & Lamoille County RS3 203, a former-Great Northern unit, works at Morrisville in 1969. During the year 1977, trains on the former-St. J were powered by Vermont Northern's decrepit ex-LIRR C420's. **At left**, blue-and-yellow 202 runs along the Lamoille River east of Morrisville, April 28, 1977.

Scott Hartley

An ex-Lehigh & Hudson River RS3 works at Morrisville in August 1975.

use for the hood-mounted smoke deflectors originally necessitated by their former high-speed passenger duties.

When the sought-after track contract went to another firm, M-K quickly lost interest in the VN, and once again the state began looking for another operator.

In late 1977, the Northern Vermont Corporation, a group whose stockholders included several major area corporations and the Central Vermont Railway, agreed to take over the St. J on New Year's Day 1978. To an Alco enthusiast, the new Lamoille Valley Railroad brought in locomotives just as exciting as those of its predecessors. The LVRC began service with four ex-D&H RS3's painted in attractive yellow-and-green. The new company has been the recipient of operating subsidies and government-funded track rehabilitation, and the St. J is in better physical condition than it has been in years.

Some of the Alcos have had their short hoods chopped, evoking loud protests from the purists, but the sound of these locomotives is still genuine 244, with all their inherent wheezing, gasping, thumping and hammering. A fifth RS3 is in operation, and the LVRC has acquired a few other Alcos to provide parts supplies. Even though the new MEC/B&M/D&H consolidation is already hurting the little railroad, the lengthy story of the St. J is far from over, and it appears that Alco locomotives will play a part in it for the coming future.

Vermont's most recent venture in the railroad business came in late 1980, with the purchase of Sam Pinsly's Montpelier & Barre. The 14-mile M&B was a fairly new company itself, having begun operations just 24 years earlier, utilizing portions of the defunct Barre & Chelsea and a Central Vermont branch.

62

Above, Lamoille Valley RS3's roll through the restored Fisher covered bridge over the Lamoille River east of Wolcott, Vt., in May 1979.

Denis E. Connell

Denis E. Connell

M&B's primary function was switching the quarries at Barre and Graniteville, and bringing heavy loaded granite flatcars down steep grades and through switchbacks to the CV connection at Montpelier Junction. Three elderly Alco S1's, and two even older EMD SW1's, all former-B&M units, normally handled all of the line's business. M&B locomotive rosters beginning in the late 1960's often listed additional units, including ex-StJ&LC RS3's, and various GE 70- and 44-tonners. Although the GE's ran from time to time, the additional engines were mostly units from other Pinsly short lines that found their way to storage in the weed-filled Montpelier yard.

As it was, quarry operators began to ship their granite by truck, and by the early 1970's it was common for the M&B to operate just a couple of times a week, with one locomotive handling the few carloads generated by other on-line customers.

Samuel Pinsly died in 1977, and it was his estate that finally received permission to abandon the money-losing property in November 1980. Upon the demise of the M&B, the State of Vermont purchased its trackage and real estate, and contracted operations to a local Designated Operator (a term created long after the state's initial rail purchases). The Washington County Railroad now runs the old M&B, with two of the former Pinsly S1's being sufficient to handle the meager business. (The M&B's two ancient SW1's were reassigned to a new Pinsly short line, the Pioneer Valley, in western Massachusetts.)

Providing an important boost to WCR's carload count is a new Bombardier, Ltd., rail car assembly plant in Barre. In 1981, the Canadian company began shipping new commuter coaches to New Jersey Transit. Bombardier has landed additional contracts for

Right, a pair of ex-D&H Alcos switch at Morrisville in 1979. **Below,** chopnose LVRC RS3's prepare to depart Central Vermont's Italy yard in St. Albans on their eastbound journey back to Morrisville, Sept. 12, 1980.

Ronald N. Johnson

A variety of Alcos have found purposeful lives on New England tourist railroads. **Above**, former B&M S3 1175 operated at Otter Valley No. 1 for that line's two years of existence. It is shown at Proctor, Vt., on July 21, 1977. **Upper right**, another B&M S3, the 1186, now operates on the Wolfeboro Railroad in New Hampshire. Ex-Portland Terminal Alcos have also been kept busy: **Below**, Conway Scenic Railroad S4 1055 brings a passenger train into the North Conway depot in August 1983. **Below right**, ex-PT S4 1061, now owned by freight hauler Bay Colony Railroad, is seen pulling tourists on the Cape Cod & Hyannis Aug. 19, 1983.

Scott Hartley

Ronald N. Johnson

Tom Nelligan

Ronald N. Johnson

commuter cars, so the Washington County just may be able to remain in the the black. In the meantime, the S1's have had blue trim and WCR's logo added to their red flanks, and fresh silver paint applied to their trucks. Thus, the chirping of Alco 539 prime movers still can be heard passing within a few yards of Vermont's State House.

Students of state governments generally consider the politics of Vermont to be far more progressive than those of New Hampshire. In the area of encouraging the survival of railroads, at least, it is true that New Hampshire didn't begin to show awareness until 12 years after its neighbor on the opposite shore of the Connecticut River.

While Vermont's government was instrumental in saving most of the abandoned Rutland Railroad in the early sixties, several once-busy Boston & Maine rail routes in the Granite State were simply allowed to return to nature.

In 1975, B&M ended operations on its 72-mile line from Concord north to Lincoln, an abandonment that would leave yet more of the state's forestry-dependent northern half without rail service.

This time the state government came to the rescue. Realizing the necessity of preserving service to on-line shippers, and more importantly, the need for the railroad if a large paper mill in Lincoln was to reopen, New Hampshire purchased the line from the B&M. The Lincoln Branch has seen a succession of designated operators. Their one common theme has been the reliance on Alco diesel locomotives.

The Wolfeboro Railroad, which had been running steam trains on another former-B&M branch in eastern New Hampshire, first took over the Lincoln line in 1976, operating it as its Central Division. WRR purchased Maine Central RS3 557, which had been retired the previous year, and the 22-year-old Alco was given an attractive blue-and-yellow paint job. During Wolfeboro's period of operation, occasional fan trips were run over the railroad, making the line more visible to fans than it was before or has been since.

The reopened mill at Lincoln closed its doors again after a few months, and when the Wolfeboro couldn't make a profit serving the line's remaining customers, it quit operation. It was succeeded by Weaver Brothers Construction Company, a firm that not only had the operating contract, but the job of rebuilding the branch's dilapidated trackage for the state. Weaver op-

Both photos, A. Thomas

Above, Wolfeboro RS3 101 is northbound at Laconia, N.H., early in 1976. The former B&M station, a registered landmark, housed the city's police department and local chamber of commerce. **Below**, Wolfeboro's 101 has become Goodwin Railroad 1, and the dark green Alco is seen leaving Lincoln, N.H., with Mt. Coolidge looming in the background, in summer 1977.

A. Thomas

Goodwin RS3 1 moves tonnage southbound along the Pemigewasset River near Woodstock, N.H., in 1977.

erated the line as the Goodwin Railroad with the RS3, and utilized a state-owned 44-tonner as well. Both were painted dark green in the same fashion as Weaver Brothers' dump trucks.

Following another closing of the Lincoln mill in 1980, and amidst government investigations of what Weaver was doing with the money that was being given the firm for track rehabilitation, the state revoked the construction company's operating contract. The line was run for a year starting in 1981 as the Southern Division of the North Stratford Railroad (see below), utilizing a former-Portland Terminal S1 which the state had purchased for use on the branch. After hearing the woos of several suitors, the state finally awarded the contract to a new company, the New England Southern, which began operations in 1982, utilizing the S1 and, as a backup, the 44-tonner. The Alco carries NES lettering on touched-up PT black-and-red colors. In 1983, the railroad operated out of its Lakeport headquarters, covering from Concord north as far as Plymouth, due to what may be the final closing of the Lincoln mill.

New Hampshire's other venture in the rail business began in 1977, when Maine Central abandoned its Beechers Falls branch. The portion of the line from the Grand Trunk connection at North Stratford, north 23 miles to Beechers Falls, Vt., was purchased by the state, and the new North Stratford Railroad began covering the line, using green ex-Maine Central S1 959 and a state-owned 44-tonner. The GE is the favored locomotive because of its fuel efficiency, but the line still sometimes generates enough traffic to overburden the little unit, and on those occasions the sound of the S1's 539 engine can be heard echoing along the northern reaches of the Connecticut River valley.

Like its northern neighbors, the Commonwealth of Massachusetts has also gotten into the railroad business. In addition to its purchases of B&M and PC commuter lines, the state government has seen the wisdom of saving rail routes facing the prospect of abandonment. And also like Vermont and New Hampshire, Massachusetts has contracted the actual running of its railroads to private operators.

Conrail's exodus from its extensive network of New England branch lines in 1982 resulted in several chunks of the ex-New Haven Railroad Old Colony Division becoming state property. Operation for this trackage for the most part has been contracted to the new Bay Colony Railroad Corporation, owned by George Bartholomew, proprietor of the narrow-gauge Edaville steam tourist railroad.

BCR also has been responsible for saving a good portion of Maine's Alco fleet. Bay Colony picked up five 1000-h.p. switchers, Portland Terminal S2 1052, S4's 1058, 1061 and 1063, and a Maine Central S4, to operate its two major routes, South Braintree-Plymouth and Middleboro-Cape Cod.

S4 1058 received a cranberry color scheme in 1982, while its sisters continued to run in Portland Terminal paint. In 1983, S2 1052 and S4's 1061 and 1063 were repainted in an attractive silver scheme, with wide yellow and orange bands across their flanks. The Maine Central unit had been purchased to provide parts, but in late 1983, BCR hoped to return it to service, renumbered 1062.

The railroad intends to make money where Penn Central and Conrail both failed, and Alco enthusiasts can hope that Schenectady-built switchers will remain part of BCR's program.

Another Conrail spin-off was the Pinsly's 21-mile Pioneer Valley, which began operations over two former-New Haven branches out of Westfield, Mass., in the summer of 1982. The PVRR's first regular locomotives were two 42-year-old ex-Montpelier & Barre EMC SW1's, but an Alco was added to the roster in late 1982 with the transfer of S2 106 from Pinsly Kentucky shortline Frankfort & Cincinnati. A year later, long-retired ex-StJ&LC RS3 203 arrived to serve as backup power, and was expected to be placed in service as soon as a new radiator could be installed.

PVRR business has been good, and the railroad seems to be succeeding in an area that Conrail claimed was unprofitable. After all these years, it will be nice to see a big Alco painted in the eye-pleasing Pinsly red, yellow and black colors.

One of New England's lesser-known railroads is Massachusetts short line Grafton & Upton, running 15 miles between Milford and a Conrail (former New York Central, ex-Boston & Albany) connection at North Grafton. The G&U is a dieselized electric line, having made the change from steeple-cab motors to GE diesels in the 1940's. Shutdown of G&U's owner and most important shipper, a large hardware company, a decade ago has hurt the railroad badly, leaving it to haul periodic loads of highway salt and building supplies.

Now an independent short line, the G&U relies on an

The latest reincarnations of the former-B&M Lincoln Branch have utilized state-owned ex-Portland Terminal S1 1008. These views during August 1982 were photographed during the line's operation as the Southern Division of the North Stratford Railroad Corporation, and prior to the takeover by the New England Southern. **Above**, the elderly S1 rolls through the weeds at Plymouth, and, at **right**, it pulls one car southbound along the shore of Pagus Bay, between Weirs and Lakeport, N.H.

Both photos, A. Thomas

S4 purchased new from Alco during better times, and a GE 44-tonner. Generally, the Alco is cranked up a couple of days a week and leaves the shelter of its Hopedale enginehouse stall to make a quick run through the quaint New England towns to the Conrail connection and back.

Another obscure Massachusetts short line is the Fore River Railroad, connecting owner General Dynamics' Quincy shipyard with Conrail at South Braintree. Since earliest days, FR had operated with a pair of anemic-looking GE 70-ton center-cab switchers. But in 1977 Alco was at last represented on the roster, in the form of an ex-Southern Pacific S6. The orange switcher became the first (and thus far, only) unit of this model in the entire Northeast. One of the GE's was retained as a backup engine until the summer of 1981, when Portland Terminal S4 1062 was purchased to provide protection power.

Happily, 251 and 539 engines are now familiar sounds through the sandlots and suburban backyards of Boston's South Shore.

The continued development of New England short lines has perpetuated the sight and sound of Alco diesels in the Northeast. But the products of Schenectady have also found caring homes with the emergence and growth of tourist lines and scenic railroads. Although these operations' primary attraction are their rosters of somewhat diminutive steam locomotives, Alco diesels have proven useful in providing standby motive power and for other purposes.

The Steamtown museum had always relied exclusively on steam to cover its train ride over 11 miles of the Green Mountain. However, new management that took over in 1980 realized the necessity of refurbishing the organization's display and operating steam locomotives, and during 1981 borrowed GMRC diesels to cover the few trains that were run. Although Steamtown owns no diesels, it soon realized the enthusiasm accorded first-generation internal-combustion power, and the museum has appealed quite successfully to Alco fans by running passenger trips behind Green Mountain's RS1's, the only examples of this model in New England.

A brief-lived tourist line was the Otter Valley, which ran trips through the marble quarries over 3½ miles of former-Clarendon & Pittsford trackage at Proctor, Vt. Powering these trains during the two years of OVRR, 1977-78, was an ex-B&M S3 painted in an unusual auburn color and carrying "ONE" in its number boards.

The Wolfeboro Railroad, which had offered steam passenger trains over a 12-mile former-B&M branch at Sanbornville, N.H., had also gained some Alco diesel experience with its freight operation of the state-owned Lincoln Branch (see page 65). During its brief tenancy on that line, WRR ran a couple of passenger trips behind blue-and-yellow RS3 101. But more recently, in 1979, the original Wolfeboro was abandoned, only to be revived under new management a year later. One of its current locomotives is ex-B&M S3 1186, painted in maroon-and-gold colors arranged similarly to the B&M's old road unit scheme.

Further north in New Hampshire another colorful Alco survives on the Conway Scenic Railroad. Former-PT S4 1055 is repainted in shiny PT black, red and

Ronald N. Johnson

A. Thomas

Above, North Stratford's S1 959 takes cars southbound through Tinkerville, N.H., en route to the GT interchange in August 1979. **Left**, the S1 is in NSRC's latest two-tone green scheme as the Alco awaits the midday arrival of the GT way freight at North Stratford.

white, and carries CSRC lettering and logos. Other diesel delights at Conway are an operating ex-Maine Central GE 44-tonner and display unit B&M F7 4266 in resplendent maroon and gold.

One other tourist operation features Alco diesels. The Cape Cod & Hyannis Railroad, which has run successful summer passenger trains on the Cape since 1981 (and has indicated possible interest in providing future commuter and intercity service under subsidy), has used a variety of borrowed switchers. Otter Valley's ex-B&M S3, now the property of a Rhode Island switching road, has carried CC&H No. 3. The company also powers its trains with Alco S's leased from Bay Colony Railroad.

In addition to all of these, speculation has run high in recent years that the management of the Valley Railroad, a steam line operating former-New Haven trackage out of Essex, Conn., will purchase and operate one of Amtrak's few remaining ex-NH RS3's. Alco enthusiasts can only hope the preservationists at the Valley realize the value (and potential audience appeal) of saving one of these historic diesels.

Tom Nelligan

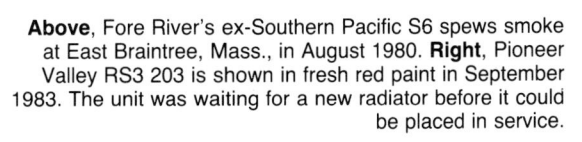

Above, Fore River's ex-Southern Pacific S6 spews smoke at East Braintree, Mass., in August 1980. **Right**, Pioneer Valley RS3 203 is shown in fresh red paint in September 1983. The unit was waiting for a new radiator before it could be placed in service.

Scott Hartley

Tom Nelligan

Grafton & Upton S4 1001 works the Conrail (ex-NYC) interchange at North Grafton, Mass., in November 1981.

Ronald N. Johnson

Scott Hartley

5/The future

As this is being written in late 1983, there are approximately 50 Alco diesels active on New England railroads. Add to that tally the operation of CP Rail's Vermont and Maine lines, Canadian National MLW's on Grand Trunk and Central Vermont, Amtrak's RS3's, D&H power on the B&M and MEC, and Long Island units helping out on Metro-North in Connecticut, and it's safe to double the number of Alcos that may be seen on any day.

That may appear to be a large number of these sought-after diesels, and perhaps it is. But remember, New England is not the tiny corner of the nation that outsiders might perceive. The distance from Greenwich, Conn., to Van Buren, Me., is roughly akin to, say, Philadelphia to Fort Wayne, or Kansas City to Pueblo. Thus, even New England's healthy allotment of Alcos is spread rather thin.

It seems safe to predict that some Alcos will be with us for several years to come. But other diesels continue to make inroads, and it will be only a matter of time before the remaining Alcos die of old age or from lack of parts. During preparation of this book, it was encouraging to note the emergence of new Alco-powered New England railroads. But at the same time, other railroads silenced their 539-, 244- and 251-fleets forever.

The only advice that can be given in this area is that which is said to all watchers of endangered species. We must enjoy New England's Alcos while we can.

Most of New England's remaining Alcos will probably remain in service until they can no longer run. Central Vermont's small fleet of RS11's make up half of that company's road-unit roster, and despite their generally poor conditions, they will be kept patched up and rolling until that far-off day when new power can be acquired. Likewise, the RS3's of Amtrak and Vermont Railway will most likely stay on the road and be retired only in instances of serious mechanical failures.

Scott Hartley

Gary Knapp

71

Happily, newer and better-maintained Alco-design diesels will continue to operate over Canadian National's and CP Rail's New England lines. CN still makes periodic locomotive purchases from Bombardier, and even though CP hasn't bought an Alco in a dozen years, the railway is well along on a program to rebuild all 69 of its remaining RS18's. But for the small marginal short lines, of which Grafton & Upton is just one of many, the future is always uncertain. Their day-to-day existences will continue and we can only hope their Alco diesels will keep running along with the railroads.